Gandhi's List of Social Sins
Lessons in Truth

by

Frank Woolever

DORRANCE PUBLISHING CO., INC.
PITTSBURGH, PENNSYLVANIA 15222

The events, people, and places herein are depicted to the best recollection of the author, who assumes complete and sole responsibility for the accuracy of this narrative.

All Rights Reserved
Copyright © 2011 by Frank Woolever

No part of this book may be reproduced or transmitted, downloaded, distributed, reverse engineered, or stored in or introduced into any information storage and retrieval system, in any form or by any means, including photocopying and recording, whether electronic or mechanical, now known or hereinafter invented without permission in writing from the publisher.

Dorrance Publishing Co., Inc.
701 Smithfield Street
Pittsburgh, PA 15222
Visit our website at www.dorrancebookstore.com

ISBN: 978-1-4349-0794-3
eISBN: 978-1-4349-5552-4

*To my parents for faith bestowed;
to my wife and daughters for their encouragement and love.*

Contents

Foreword by Jerome Berrigan xi

Introduction: Gandhi's List of Social Sins xv
Satyagraha
The Power of the Printed Word

One: Wealth Without Work 1
A Perspective on Wealth
New Deal
Prison Labor
Wealth Distribution
The Healing Value of Ordinary Labor

Two: Pleasure Without Conscience 16
Fasting
Prison Insights
Chavez's Witness
Gandhi's Reflections

Three: Commerce Without Morality 35
Indian Home Rule
Nicaraguan Model
Maritime Entanglements

Effects on Indigenous Populations
Liberation Theology
March to the Sea

Four: Science Without Humanity 56
Pacifist Evolution
Means and Ends
Pax Christi
Nuclear Shadow
Violence Begets Violence
Behind Bars

Five: Knowledge Without Character 78
Assessing the Law
A Monastic Reflection
Champion for the Downtrodden
A Handful of Dreams
Social Stigmas
Indomitable Spirit

Six: Worship Without Sacrifice 95
Religious Reformer
Fasting for the Untouchables
Noncooperation
El Salvador
Seamless Garment
Jewish Concerns
Worship and Sacrifice in Prison

Seven: Politics Without Principle 122
Martin Luther King Jr.'s Tribute
Bridging Hindu-Muslim Tensions
Jubilee Justice
Mediation
Key and Bolt

Judicial Discretion
Political Perspectives
Gandhi's Heartbreak
Fateful War Decisions

Eight: Final Word 145
Sources 151

Acknowledgements

Special thanks to Heidi Woolever Daly and Meme Woolever for their invaluable suggestions and editing assistance. Amy Drew Woolever and Daniel Krainin uncovered many of my past letters to the editor, giving this effort some momentum. Thanks also to Ned Daly who added valuable consultation. John F. Clifford, revered family friend and surrogate grandfather to our daughters, drew the cover sketch. The foreword by Jerome Berrigan, crafted out of love and respect for Gandhi, is deeply appreciated.

In the process of my research I was fortunate to meet with Arun Gandhi, founder of the M.K. Gandhi Institute for Non-Violence at the University of Rochester, who shared with me some of his personal experiences with his grandfather. Arun has been a rich source of information about his family members, including his grandmother Kastur, Gandhi's wife of sixty-two years. (Arun and his wife, Sunanda Gandhi, coauthored with Carol Lynn Yellin a book about Kastur, *The Forgotten Woman*, which was published in 1998 in concurrence with the 50th anniversary of Gandhi's assassination.)

A thanks for permission to reprint the photographs and political cartoons in this book is extended to GandhiServe—a charitable foundation aiming to promote the life and work of Mahatma Gandhi. In addition to providing educational programs, GandhiServe Foundation works to safeguard and distribute documents, photographs, and films relating to Gandhi and the Indian independence movement. Its archive is the largest of its kind outside India and, along with further details about the foundation; it can be viewed online at www.gandhiserve.org.

Foreword

I take it as a personal tribute to have been asked by a long-time friend, Frank Woolever, to pen an introduction to his study of Mahatma Gandhi. Frank is himself responding to a great and noble tradition in his attempt to widen and deepen the influence of so truly a deathless figure as Gandhi to benefit those who might not have learned of him.

Living in a time of history, when warfare and interpersonal violence are out of control across the world, Frank has chosen the living example of Gandhi, who was selected as the basis of his teaching: AHIMSA, "freedom from every form of domination and aggression." The central note of his reliance on ahimsa is Satyagraha or truth force or nonviolence. This reality, Gandhi reverently urged as "the greatest force at the disposal of any person…more powerful indeed than the mightiest weapon ever devised by human ingenuity." (Indeed, it truly is.)

The American civil rights and political leader, Martin Luther King Jr., is known as an admirer and imitator of Gandhi. King said, "Hatred is never quelled by hatred in this world…" Such a sentiment, by so authentic a moral authority as King, exposes to timeless view the attack on Afghanistan, a war of naked revenge initiated by President Bush as an aftermath of 9/11.

Not only does King deny forever the value of recrimination as a worthy human aspiration but also grew to realize that he personally must begin to change the nature of his own world by submitting to violence rather than ever consciously wishing it upon an attacker or an enemy.

Returning now to Mahatma Gandhi as subject of Frank Woolever's study, we find ourselves beginning to share in Frank's esteem for this great native of India. As an impressive example, we hear Gandhi's words questioning the total reliance of Western education from the lowest to the highest degree on the brain, the mind, the organ of calculation, and the faculty of measurement to solve any problem: mathematical, historical, or philosophical. Gandhi anguished at the plight of India's caste of untouchables, yearned to offer them the freedom that their humanity absolutely required. He came to see that a solution was possible only if those in authority could be moved by compassion on India, and the abysmal state of the millions of downtrodden people. Gandhi said, "If you want something important to be done, you must not merely satisfy the reason. You must satisfy the heart also. The penetration of the heart comes from suffering, which opens the inner understanding of men and women…"

I believe that Frank Woolever felt the need and the urgency to interpret the mind and heart of Gandhi, whom he esteemed as one who believed and lived as he himself aspired to do. Many times, Gandhi resisted unjust laws by submitting to prison; Frank, likewise, violated a law enacted merely to bolster United States governmental authority in Third-World countries; a law that criminally caused death to innocent people. He reluctantly suffered a period of jail staying. Gandhi taught that the very spirit of peacemaking lay in one's willingness to choose voluntary suffering, plus a sacrifice of one's freedom. While in jail, and afterward as well, Frank has interpreted Gandhi's love of creation to certify his own concern for the well being of the Earth and the environment.

A distinct quality of Frank Woolever's writing is its gentleness and lack of assertiveness. In his verbal structures, there is a near tentativeness, as though he were saying, "Likely, you have heard and read this before; excuse me for repeating it. I am hopeful that you can grasp its inner meaning." Above all, implicit to Frank's text is the idea: "I sow seeds only; the fruits are up to God."

Here, perhaps, is a question that needs to be asked: from what wellspring, from what source or origin did Gandhi himself draw inspiration for his life of leadership and resistance? Initially, from the BHAVAGAD GITA, the Hindu bible; from it, Gandhi quoted, "…nonviolence succeeds only when it springs from a real, living faith in God." Speaking of this passage, Gandhi said further, "The means may be compared to seeds; the end, to a tree. And between the means (belief in the truth) and the end (free adaptation of nonviolence for life), there is the same inviolable connection as there is between the seed and the tree."

Having said that, I have said enough. And now, I invite you, together with Frank Woolever, to accept a fruitful and loving union with Mahatma Gandhi.

Design: © GhandiServe Foundation—www.gandhiserve.org
Photo: Kanu Gandhi/GandhiServe

Introduction

In 2007, the United Nations General Assembly declared October 2nd the International Day of Non-Violence in recognition of the birthday of Mohandas Gandhi, also known as *Mahatma* (great soul). Like many, I had long admired this man of peace, so often pictured in his simple loincloth. Like many, I had seen *Gandhi*, the film that brought portions of his life story onto large screens around the world. Yet it was not until I went to prison for three months that I seriously began to explore the life and impact of this complicated, holy man.

In November 2005, along with thirty-nine other protesters, I made the conscious choice to cross the line onto the army base at Fort Benning, Georgia. The following spring, I was incarcerated in Canaan Federal Prison Camp, a low-security prison near Scranton, Pennsylvania, as a punishment for civil disobedience.

Some understanding of the reasons behind my decision to climb under a fence and get arrested, an act that had been previously undertaken by more than a dozen others from my region in Central New York, might be helpful. Protests at the gates of the School of the Americas (S.O.A.) in Ft. Benning began in 1990, one year after six Jesuit priests, their housekeeper, and her daughter were brutally murdered in El Salvador. Nineteen graduates of the S.O.A. were later implicated in the deadly attack. The first year the vigil drew only a handful of protesters, but word began to spread. Each year on the weekend before Thanksgiving more people joined in the effort to call attention to the activities inside the fences and gates. Hundreds, then thousands began arriving from all over the United States and Latin America. For several years, my wife and I joined the protests and we watched the number of participants grow from year to year. Young people, especially from Jesuit colleges and high schools, came in droves, and priests, ministers, and religious women were always present. On Sunday morning a solemn procession passes in front of the gates as the name of every known dead or wounded victim of an S.O.A. graduate is chanted individually over a loudspeaker. It has been, for many, a powerful religious and ecumenical experience. When I was arrested in 2005, more than 19,000 people were gathered at the gates. Since 2000, more than two hundred nonviolent protesters have received jail sentences for symbolically trespassing onto the base in what has been rightly called a Gandhian wave.

In 1993, after Newsweek published an article about the S.O.A. titled "Running a School for Dictators," Congress began to question its necessity. The House of Representatives has come close to cutting off funding, but the school is still operating. Training manuals, uncovered in 1996 through the Freedom of Information Act, document the illegal torture techniques taught to military and police personnel. Murders and coercive repression have been repeatedly traced to graduates of the institution. This continues today. In 2000, due to public awareness of the training manuals, Congress decided to change the name of the school to the Western Hemisphere Institute for Security Cooperation (WHINSEC). In this book, the institution is referred to as the S.O.A.

Writer Naomi Klein traced the history of the school and its legacy in a 2005 article for *The Nation*. It was founded and operated in Panama until 1984, when it was moved to Ft. Benning. Many Central and South America countries have sent military and civilian personnel to learn tactics in control. Repressive governments have been especially drawn to this arrangement. The school became notorious and infamous in Latin America as graduates returned to their respective countries to abuse, torture, and murder at the behest of dictators and other authority figures, who tended to be friendly to United States commercial and anti-communist interests'. According to the group SOA Watch:

> Over its 59 years, the SOA has trained over 60,000 Latin American soldiers in counterinsurgency techniques, sniper training, commando and psychological warfare, military intelligence and interrogation tactics. These graduates have consistently used their skills to wage a war against their own people. Among those targeted by SOA graduates are educators, union organizers, religious workers, student leaders and others who work for the rights of the poor. Hundreds of thousands of Latin Americans have been tortured, raped, assassinated, 'disappeared,' (and) massacred.

Klein notes that within the S.O.A. lay the roots of the 2004 torture scandal. The disclosure of terror techniques used by U.S. soldiers in Abu Ghraib and Guantanamo prisons shocked the world. The shame of these revelations brought an apology from the United States government; it gave the impression that only a few misguided soldiers were involved, mostly of lower rank. Klein's article gives historical perspective to torture as policy, tracing it back to the beginning of the S.O.A. at the end of World War II. It is only selective amnesia, according to Klein, that allows us to believe that these recent acts of torture are isolated. The United States military has been linked to them for at least the past half century.

In Canaan Federal Prison Camp, I was allowed to keep five books at a time. One that I had sent to me was *In the Footsteps of Gandhi: Conversations with Spiritual Social Activists* by Catherine Graham, which my daughter had given me as a Christmas gift. It contains interviews with individuals who give personal tribute to Gandhi for affecting their own spirituality and social action. Among those included are significant justice seekers of our time, including Desmond Tutu, Thich Nhat Hanh, and Cesar Chavez. Arun Gandhi, grandson of Mohandas Gandhi, wrote the foreword. As a youth Arun had been given a list of seven social sins by his paternal grandfather who strongly believed that they were at the root of violence in our world. The list originated with a reader of *Young India*, one of Gandhi's newspapers, in which it was first published in October 1925.

The concept of a "social" sin may seem unusual regardless of religious beliefs. From a Christian perspective, religious education has focused heavily on individual faults. Many people can repeat from memory the seven capital sins: pride, avarice, envy, wrath, lust, gluttony, and sloth. Historically, they have been taught as personal failings. From Catholic social teachings, the collective dimensions of relationships have emerged over the past century. These come from documents of a hierarchical nature, mainly from papal encyclicals and bishops' conferences; they are not always well known among the Catholic laity. Yet these texts have been important statements for many Catholic and Protestant theologians, as well as Jewish scholars, and have had an impact on various political decisions and laws. Placing them in perspective within the context of Gandhi's list of social sins gives broader insight into some of the critical issues of our time, including the recognition that social structures can be sinful.

Satyagraha

Gandhi began his work as an activist in South Africa. In 1893, at the age of twenty-three, Gandhi left India soon after returning from his studies in London, and went to South Africa to work as a lawyer. In short order he experienced a form of racial prejudice previously unknown to him in either India or London. Gandhi encountered a rude beginning on his first railroad trip when a white man complained about his presence in the first-class compartment for which he had purchased a ticket. He refused to ride third class:

> 'I tell you, I was permitted to travel in this compartment at Durban and I insist on going on in it.'
> 'No you won't,' said the official. You must leave this compartment or else I shall have to call a police constable to push you out'
> 'Yes you may. I refuse to get out voluntarily.'
> The constable came. He took me by the hand and forced me out. My luggage was also taken out…and the train steamed away. I went and sat in the waiting room…It was winter, and winter in the higher regions of South Africa is severely cold.

Gandhi waited all night for another train, pondering his experience as a victim of racism. As he traveled onward to Pretoria he was further insulted and even beaten. This trip was a turning point in his life; he questioned if he should remain in South Africa to complete his legal work and confront the "deep disease of color prejudice."

Gandhi had come to South Africa to represent an Indian merchant in a legal case. The proceedings were delayed by litigation; nevertheless both sides were satisfied after Gandhi negotiated a careful settlement. Gandhi, out of concern that the opposing party would go bankrupt, worked out a long-term repayment plan. His approach to law for the rest of his life was to unite the opposing sides for the best possible outcome.

Once established in his legal work in Pretoria, Gandhi, being a professional, fit into society without much difficulty. Yet he came to understand the plight of the majority of Indians in his new surroundings who had little knowledge or experience in dealing with the racist systems they encountered. Gandhi set out to listen to their stories. In the second half of the 19th century, most Indians in South Africa had arrived on crowded ships as indentured workers. They lived under an agreement that after five years of work they would either receive money for a trip home or be granted permission to stay in South Africa as free Indians. In the first year, laborers were paid ten shillings, about $2.50 a month, with an additional shilling for each month thereafter. For those who remained after five years the freedom was illusionary; most Indians found themselves stuck in semi-slavery conditions, along with other non-white residents, and considered *coolies* by the British and the Dutch. Ironically, many were Untouchables who likely signed up thinking they would find a better life outside the caste system.

After Gandhi's first year in South Africa, the original conditions for low income Indians were altered. Under new legislation, if after the five-year period indentured Indian workers wished to stay, they had to pay three pounds for themselves and each dependent. As an indentured worker, it took six months to earn three pounds. This new tax drew Gandhi into action and he began to organize against the changes. He quickly became an effective and well-known leader among the Indian population. Once Gandhi realized that he had years of work ahead of him in South Africa, he returned to India to gather his immediate family and bring them back with him. On their return voyage, in 1896, they arrived on one of two coolie ships filled with eight hundred free Indians.

Gandhi was already in the public eye, as remarks he had made in India about conditions in South Africa had been publicized and exaggerated by the South African media, and a mob was formed to receive him. Once Gandhi saw that he was not able to leave the ship, he sent his family off the boat ahead of him. When he finally disembarked, he was beaten to the point of fainting. The local police chief's wife helped rescue him by sheltering him behind her parasol, bravely standing between him and the frenzied mob, until the police were able to help him escape and reunite with his family. As an expression of Gandhi's developing nonviolent philosophy, he refused to press criminal charges against his assailants.

At this time, the treatment and laws of Indian residents varied from province to province. In the Orange State, Indians had been largely driven out. In the Transvaal, Indians were the victims of especially hateful discrimination and were only allowed to live and own property in certain areas. In Nataal, new immigration requirements included passing a test in a European language to gain residency. Restrictions on Indian merchants were widespread across South Africa.

In 1906 the inspiration for nonviolent, grass roots action began to emerge in Gandhi's mind as punitive legislative proposals affecting the Indian population were under consideration. The Asiatic Registration Act, known as the Black Act because of its racial intent, mandated the registration of all Indians above the age of eight in the Transvaal region, whether indentured laborers, merchants, or those with professional skills. Gandhi saw the potential consequences of this and perceived that, once the act was implemented, it would soon be expanded to include the entire country. He was chosen by Indians in South Africa to go to London to argue against what they viewed as nefarious legislation. In his first trip back to England since law school, Gandhi initially thought he had succeeded in persuading the British government to withhold agreement on its passage. However, upon his return to South Africa, he found that he had been tricked. The Transvaal government could subsequently act on its own to put the law into effect. They did so, with implementation set for July 31, 1907.

Under Gandhi's guidance, a passive resistance movement was initiated. The new law said that those who failed to register were subjected to arrest and imprisonment. Gandhi did not register, was prosecuted under this statute, and received a two-month sentence, his first incarceration. He worried that he would be alone in this effort, but soon a hundred and fifty fellow Indians joined him in the same prison.

In *Indian Opinion*, a weekly journal that Gandhi incorporated into his ashram, he asked for ideas to name this new resistance movement. One suggestion was *sadagraha* (firmness in a good cause), which Gandhi modified to *satyagraha* (truth force). It was conceived as a force not of brute strength but a soul force, a force of nonviolence. Gandhi developed his philosophy of satyagraha over his years in South Africa.

As the satyagraha campaign proceeded in the Transvaal, the government raised the ante. A three-pound tax was added on laborers who had arrived in South Africa as indentured, but who had earned their freedom after a period of labor. This substantial new tax infuriated Indians. Then, a justice of the Supreme Court invalidated marriages not performed in Christian rites or recorded with the Register of Marriages, which Indian marriages were not. This discrimination helped bring women into the satyagraha campaign. In one year, Gandhi or one of his sons was arrested eight times. By the end of the five-year struggle to defeat the Black Act, members of Gandhi's family had served eighteen jail terms.

Through Gandhi's careful negotiation with his adversary, General Jan Christiaan Smuts, a compromise emerged. In July 1914, the Indian Relief Bill became law, which pleased both sides. Hindu, Muslim, and Parsi marriages were declared valid, and the three-pound tax was abolished. The repeal of the racist component of the legislation was a victory for all the Indians in South

Africa. It was also the vindication of a resistance movement. It was now time for Gandhi to bring his insight and experience back with him to India.

Gandhi's personal discipline was an inspiration to those who knew him. He went to prison again and again, both in South Africa and later in India as part of his satyagraha protests. His actions were always carried out in a nonviolent manner, and he insisted upon this discipline for those who wished to join in his efforts. Inspired by Gandhi's leadership and witness, thousands of individuals were willing to go to prison for causes they newly believed in. Gandhi was never accused of having a lack of courage. He never wavered on the importance of this virtue and tried to foster it in every volunteer for every satyagraha effort. Yet Gandhi admitted that he often contradicted himself, and that he was not always consistent. When deciding upon and weighing possible reactions to various satyagraha actions, he often labored over them. He took his time making important decisions, even when his followers became impatient. Sometimes, exhaustion and even physical illness gave a hint of his internal struggle in settling upon or carrying out collective actions. Gandhi often questioned himself and the purity of his choices in various campaigns.

Gandhi returned to India in 1915, after working for twenty years in South Africa, and thus began the second stage of his work. Although India was under colonial rule, the issues were very different than those he had faced in South Africa. Before colonization in 1757, India had supported a thriving merchant class. Weavers and spinners produced fine clothing and other creative textiles. However, once under British control, the East India Company set rules that caused widespread impoverishment of the Indian population. As Britain's textile industry at home grew, the East India Company, consisting essentially of middlemen, did the bidding of the colonizers. As they brought British goods into India, the ruling authorities stifled competition from Indian artisans or merchants. The East India Company overpowered the creative forces of centuries of Indian experience, thus affecting the nation's identity as well as its financial well-being. In 1857, the British Raj took control of the administrative affairs of India. Gandhi came to understand that the ruin of India by British colonizers was virtually total: economic, political, cultural, and spiritual.

In time, under Gandhi's guidance, for both practical and symbolic reasons the spinning wheel returned to widespread use across India. The implications of this were great; Jawaharlal Nehru, the first prime minister of independent India, said that Gandhi had given India back its identity.

Gandhi recognized the importance of getting his message out to a wide audience. In his first efforts at organizing in South Africa he began *Indian Opinion*. When he returned to India, he started the English language *Young India*. Twenty years later, after the British government shut down that publication, he began another weekly journal, *Harijan* (Child of God), with a focus on the issue of Untouchables, and published it in three languages: English, Hindi and Gujarati. Of financial necessity, Gandhi's various publications were limited in circulation, but the mainstream media often reprinted his articles.

The Power of the Printed Word

The inclusion of letters to the editor in this book speaks to my respect for the power of the written word. As the son of a newspaperman and the grandson of a newspaper printer and typesetter (a skilled job that has largely been lost in the transition to computer technology), I share in Gandhi's appreciation of the press. One of my daughters, teaching in a public high school in Washington DC, had the task of working with a group of students to restart the school newspaper which had been defunct for several years. She exposed her students to a number of professional settings, including visits to the *Washington Post*. Once she asked me to visit as a guest lecturer, with a focus on writing letters to the editor. My basic message to them was the power of published writing. When *The Rainbow* was reestablished and the first edition distributed, she sent me a copy. It was a pleasure to look on the masthead and see what the journalism class had chosen for the paper's new slogan - THE POWER OF THE PRINTED WORD.

Following my release from Canaan Federal Prison Camp, I wrote eight articles for the Syracuse diocesan newspaper *The Catholic Sun*. In these commentaries I used the framework of the social sins to reflect on my prison experience. As I researched the literature, I found little information on the seven social sins. It seemed reasonable to give them more exposure and so I began the process of writing this book. I revisited my well-worn copy of The *Essential Gandhi*, edited by Louis Fischer, and searched for more information at the library.

The purpose of this book is threefold. First, it will give greater exposure to the list of social sins, largely unknown in Western culture. Second, this book will explore how Gandhi's life and efforts can be a useful guide in considering the intersection of morality, politics, and religion inside the United States as well as in a global context. Each chapter explains how Gandhi's thoughts and actions relate to various aspects of contemporary life. Third, this book provides an opportunity for me to share some of my own reflections and experiences in relation to the seven social sins.

While my own prison time was limited, Gandhi was imprisoned for a cumulative total of six years. Because of the Mahatma's willingness to sacrifice, his life story and his teachings have affected peacemakers of every nationality and religion. Therefore, Gandhi's recognition of the social sins as causes of violence deserves our attention. In the end, I hope that the reader will grow in appreciation of Gandhi's challenges and responses. He avoided attacking individuals, either verbally or in writing, often going out of his way to relate to his adversaries. Gandhi held no personal hatred against his opponents.

Some common Indian words that appear in this book have concepts that are readily understandable, such as *ahimsa* (doing no harm), and satyagraha. Indian proper names are at times adjusted due to marriage or familiarity. For example, Kastur, the wife of Gandhi, was also called Kasturba, Mother Kastur, or sometimes-just Ba. Gandhi was called *Bapu* (father) by those closest to him. As a mark of warmth and respect, friends, associates, and the Indian population often attached a *ji* to the end of his name, as in Gandhiji.

India gained her independence on August 15, 1947. Gandhi was assassinated in January 1948 at the age of seventy-eight.

Gandhi in the Lion's Den; *Simplicissimus*, Munich (Germany)—Copyright: Vithalbhal Jhavert/Gandhi Server—KW: Mahatma Gandhi

Simplicissimus was a weekly devoted to international affairs published in Munich in the early 1930s. One of its political cartoons shows Gandhi spinning a peaceful protest against Britain's denial of self-rule to India while the British rulers, depicted as imperial lions, look on in anger and bewilderment. (1931)

One

Wealth Without Work

"We should spin, therefore, if only to guard against the pernicious tendency of regarding the toilers as being low on the social scale. Spinning is therefore as obligatory on the prince as on the peasant." —Gandhi

One of Gandhi's core beliefs was that working with one's hands is essential to a person's moral development. While Gandhi was esteemed for his work fighting racism, ethnic discrimination and colonialism, he reminded readers of his weekly publications that he kept his balance by spinning and raising food. He began two farming communities in South Africa and three ashrams in India after his permanent return there.

Where did the idea to farm and the importance of working with one's hands come from? As a preface to understanding this question, it is important to note that throughout his life Gandhi could be very impulsive. When he was intellectually and spiritually convinced that an idea was sound, he did not hesitate to pursue its application, sometimes very quickly. This was the case when he decided to start a farm immediately after reading *Unto This Last*, by John Ruskin, on an overnight train. Ruskin addressed pervasive materialism and unwholesome competition in

19th century England and stressed the dignity of human labor, including working with one's hands, an idea that Gandhi took very seriously. Ruskin believed that the true basis of society was not wealth, but rather human companionships and relationships that he called "invisible gold," the principle motives that rule human life. He held that the rich should eschew luxuries until everyone has enough to meet basic needs.

Gandhi had been practicing law successfully in South Africa for eight years before he purchased his first farm, the Phoenix Settlement. He was doing very well financially when he read *Unto This Last*, yet he had such a strong emotional response to Ruskin's book that he almost immediately changed his lifestyle and moved his family to the farm. Likeminded others soon followed. Gandhi proudly noted that at Phoenix "everything…from cooking to scavenging was done with our own hands." Community members adjusted to life where all tasks were done cooperatively, from building simple living structures to cleaning dishes. They learned by doing. Gandhi placed increasing importance on manual labor throughout his life, he perceived that a measure of working with one's hands on a daily basis had a spiritual dimension. In the early years of the farm, Gandhi participated in the daily farm work as much as possible, although his law practice and civil rights concerns consumed much of his time. At this point in his life, his energy was focused on Indian families and small farmers who were suffering under the restrictive legislation of the Transvaal Provincial Government.

Seven years after founding Phoenix, as the political pressure increased on both indentured and free Indians, Gandhi started a second community closer to Johannesburg, the Transvaal capital, on an 1100-acre property owned by his German-Jewish friend Herman Kallenbach. Gandhi named it Tolstoy Farm because of his admiration for Leo Tolstoy. To concentrate his efforts on public service and to share in the life of the farm, he eventually handed over his legal duties to his colleagues.

The Phoenix Settlement and Tolstoy Farm were not called ashrams, although they were similar to the ashrams Gandhi later founded in India. An ashram is like a personal hermitage. For Gandhi, his family, close friends, and coworkers it was where they made their home in a spirit of prayer, service, and farm life. Ashrams have ancient roots in India. They have been used as religious retreats, especially for monks, as well as places of pilgrimage for the Indian populace. They are traditionally havens for renunciation of worldly pleasures. Gandhi's ashrams, however, were not places of withdrawal from the world, but places of reflection and training in preparation for engagement with the world. As a lawyer, Gandhi obviously respected formal education, yet he did not like the biases within the academic world that favored those with more resources. To that end, he himself was the teacher of his sons and the other children of Tolstoy Farm.

Gandhi derived inspiration for some of the structure and communal rules in his ashrams from a Trappist monastery he visited in South Africa, where the monks' work, skills, structure and prayer impressed him. The silence of the monks was another dimension of monastic life that appealed to Gandhi.

A Perspective on Wealth

Each of us has our own personal reflection on the subject of wealth and income disparity. Mine is conditioned by my upbringing, the socio-economic conditions of the time, and family relationships. Coming in to the world in the very heart of the depression, my view of wealth differs from my friends who entered life in more prosperous times. In March 1933, Franklin D. Roosevelt was sworn in as president. Fearful of economic disaster, one of his first decisions was to close the banks. While the banks were closed for five days, I was born.

In my youth our family was one of modest means, existing on my father's salary as a reporter, and later as sports editor of a Syracuse paper. My mother, valedictorian of her high-school class, always remained home to raise my two sisters and me. To the best of my knowledge, we never thought much about money. We knew we were not wealthy. A second-hand car was one outward symbol of our economic condition. Yet, we thought little about it. Even before our teen years, my sisters and I always had jobs of one sort or another. That was taken for granted and considered the norm for that time period. We also learned to appreciate work. I never gave much thought to our family becoming wealthy; we were rich in other ways, especially in mutual family love. Yet, compared to the indentured workers in poverty in South Africa or the rural poor in villages across India, our family was very wealthy indeed.

New Deal

The most successful job program in American history was the New Deal, created during Franklin D. Roosevelt's first term. The United States was experiencing a deep economic depression, with roots that became exposed in the economic crash of 1929. Part of Roosevelt's social legislation put unemployed workers back into the labor market using construction and cultural projects, including the Civilian Conservation Corps (CCC) and the Works Progress Administration (WPA). Monuments to those efforts, including bridges, buildings, and murals still remain in American cities and rural areas. The effect of these programs was to get unemployed people back on track, monetarily and psychologically, through the opportunity to do meaningful work.

Another component of the New Deal was the Social Security Act (1935), which created a national insurance system in which workers and employers contribute and, in time, receive benefits. It was not intended to make individuals wealthy, but to supply basic sustenance when a person retires or is no longer able to work for one reason or another. This program faced a challenge in 2005 when ideas about changing the system or adapting it to individual, personal accounts surfaced. In response to this issue, I wrote a letter, titled "Messing With Success," which was published by the Syracuse Post Standard:

> One of the principal motives behind the development of our Social Security System was the common good. This essential underpinning seems to have gotten lost in the current debate on the subject. In fact, it appears to be under attack.
>
> Based on the framework of mandatory payroll contributions, the Social Security System was a social contract between the government and the public at large. It provided a safety net, especially for the poor and disabled in society, and it addressed the critical issue of unemployment during those difficult economic times. One reason

that citizens have supported it through the years has been in the recognition that it serves the common good.

It appears that our president is now trying to shift the focus of Social Security away from a common interest to an individual perspective, while making an appeal, as such, to younger citizens born after 1949. Yet, they, too, need to know the basic values behind this bedrock piece of social policy.

In a book entitled *The Common Interest*, Leslie Dunbar, without minimizing the need to address economic constraints and adjustments stresses the larger picture that we as a nation must not forget, 'The Social Security System, as conceived by the planners of the New Deal, is a great civic bond. It may always stand in need of maintenance. But weakening the bond created by that act of marvelous statesmanship would also weaken the good order of this society.'

Prison Labor

In the American economy, a top heavy system of rewards exists that most workers believe has reached obscene proportions. The story of one of my fellow inmates at Canaan exemplifies this unbalanced system. Charlie (not his real name) was an exceptionally hard worker in the prison-camp setting. His knowledge of landscaping, together with his initiative in suggesting and carrying out projects on prison grounds, earned him recognition all the way to the warden. Still, he received only an inmate's small, hourly wage. Most of the inmates working on the landscape detail were making twelve cents an hour, and I have no reason to think that his pay was any higher.

Before incarceration Charlie was a day trader in the Midwest. However, he got into trouble when investors asked him to handle their portfolios. Charlie's career ended abruptly when a client requested his money back on short notice and he could not produce it. While the judge sympathized with him, the sentence he received did not reflect this empathy. Inside prison, instead of making a large amount of money in a short period of time, which he had done on a regular basis, he was working hard for "peanuts." Yet, he appreciated the work and was valued by the administration. Charlie had no choice but to switch from a profession where he could and did accumulate a considerable amount of wealth with almost no physical effort, to a situation where he expended an immense amount of physical labor for extremely little financial reward. The extremes of what a person's work is considered to be worth are visible in this example.

In my professional role in later life as a pastoral counselor, I was fortunate to work with a cooperative administrator at the local penitentiary. After she was promoted to New York State Commissioner of Corrections, I sent her a letter:

> In completing my doctoral work at Colgate Rochester Divinity School, I wrote my dissertation on the criminal

justice system, with special focus on the family and correction. One subject area that attracts me is the lack of ecological connection for the prisoners. In the not-too-distant past, prisons had farms, where produce was grown to help feed the population; some had dairy herds. These seemed very sensible, not only for the practical purposes of providing food but also the therapeutic benefit of working with the land and animals for the prisoners. Somewhere along the line, a major decision was made (or maybe many minor ones) to reverse this pattern. I would like to know the history of these decisions, especially the thinking behind them. With the number of farms now abandoned or going under in our state, perhaps, it is time to take a fresh look at the situation.

The commissioner, who as a warden at a county correctional facility had once overseen a greenhouse that functioned with inmate labor, responded with interest to this request. She advised me on whom to contact in the state system for more information. Although I followed up, my inquiries led to no practical results. To this day, there seems to be little movement in the direction of productive land use on prison grounds. This became even more obvious to me during my own federal imprisonment.

Dr. Urie Bronfenbrenner, an esteemed professor of Human Development and Family Studies at Cornell University, with whom I worked on a cross-cultural, human development project, told me a story about his own childhood. His father was a medical doctor, and the family lived within the confines of a state institution for the "feebleminded," which, during Bronfenbrenner's youth, was a three thousand-acre farm. The farm raised chickens and supported carpenter shops and a bakery. Bronfenbrenner sadly recalled that all these activities were eliminated by court order for encompassing a form of involuntary servitude. This same rationale may be part of the reason why our prison systems has largely moved away from farming opportunities.

Wealth Distribution

Upon returning to India in 1915, Gandhi chose a location close to the industrial city of Ahmadabad for his first ashram. Ahmadabad was a center for textile production, and weaving mills were part of the economic and cultural scene. Gandhi was friendly with some of the mill owners and members of their families. However, when a strike was called, his sympathies were with the workers. With the goal of negotiating a settlement, Gandhi helped lead daily rallies to support the strikers. From the beginning he urged arbitration, but the factory owners refused. The strike dragged on for three weeks. Gandhi's first public fast in India was an effort to encourage the textile workers to continue the strike in a nonviolent manner. His announcement that he would fast until the strike was settled caught everyone by surprise. The dynamics of this situation were personally challenging for Gandhi, since he was a special friend of the largest textile manufacturer, Ambalal Sarabhai. To complicate matters further, Sarabhai's sister Anasuya was a follower of Gandhi, and she supported the workers. After Gandhi's sudden fasting announcement, she said that she would fast with him, but he discouraged it. Three days into his fast, the impasse ended when the owners agreed to arbitration.

The principal of arbitration was essential to Gandhi as a nonviolent way to settle disputes. Almost thirty years later, in 1936, the mill owners' association asked the textile labor union to accept a twenty percent wage cut, citing foreign competition and the worldwide economic depression. After studying the matter Gandhi suggested that: "No cut should be made till the mills have ceased to make any profit and are obliged to fall back on their capital for continuing the industry." Furthermore, Gandhi believed that information about business decisions should be shared; he regarded workers as equals to shareholders, and as such, said that they should have every right to knowledge about the transactions of their employers.

In Gandhi's approach to arbitration, unions and cooperatives recognize that workers have an obligation to pull together and support the work at hand and their employer. Mutual support between labor and management continues to be an important element in the workplace. Labor unions are one group that has traditionally addressed the dynamic of work and reward. The idea of allowing workers to have a share in the profits, through worker ownership, is finding greater acceptance and has allowed some businesses to continue despite difficult financial times.

If the capital and labor system of the United States followed the Gandhian principles of profit sharing and mediation, today's market would be quite different. In examining the concept of wealth without work, it is easy to recognize that the idea of labor has vastly changed, even since the time of Gandhi's writing. The current system of awarding enormous wages and bonuses to executives, especially CEO's in many large corporations extend far beyond what most working people consider rational boundaries. According to the Institute for Policy Studies, CEOs made 431 times as much as the average worker in 2004. This was a jump from 2001, when the ratio was 301:1. While many families struggle to get by on a minimum wage, the gap between the rich and the poor is ever widening. Meanwhile, minimum wage legislation in the United States sat unattended in Congress for over ten years as the cost of living continued to rise. Beginning in 2007, small federal adjustments have begun to adjust this discrepancy. In 2010, the wealthiest one percent of Americans possessed a greater collective net worth than the bottom ninety percent. Internationally, the trend is no different. The Archbishop of Quebec City, Maurice Couture, citing that the wealth of the richest 358 people on the planet equals the total amount held by the poorest 2.3 billion, or forty-five percent of the world's population, said that "to be poor is a kind of social apartheid."

Another concept favored by Gandhi was limiting inheritance, which would have a major impact on how individuals and communities perceive wealth. Gandhi accepted the idea of private property and a person's right to accumulate wealth. However, when a person of financial means died, he believed the estate should be left to the community. Personal wealth would not be passed on. If such a plan were adopted, even in a modified form, what a change would occur in every person's outlook! Gandhi did have many rich friends, like some of the mill owners, who supported his causes throughout his life and whom he encouraged to share their bounty while they were still alive.

★★★

Family farms drove the early economy of the United States. This self-sufficient way of life and its culture of neighborly values embraced many of Ruskin's ideas. Today, the increasing dominance of corporate agriculture threatens small-scale food production, as the United States has moved further and further away from this model. Federal subsidies enrich farmers and corporations who are already profitable. The dynamic issue of immigrant and migrant labor may also contribute to the demise of non-industrial farming in some areas, since many migrant laborers assist in the short-term needs of farms. Without such assistance, many smaller farms are unable to make ends meet.

Gandhi believed that honest labor should be esteemed and rewarded. He embraced the notion of "bread labor," the term he coined to refer to the heavy, rough work necessary to protect and provide for the basic needs of humanity. This type of work brings its own gratification, yet it is easily overlooked. For those whose work is not active, Gandhi suggested that doing physical labor, even for a half hour every day, is beneficial if one is striving for spiritual and psychological health and well-being. The rewards are greater than the effort expended.

In examining the concept of wealth without work, it is evident that the subject touches a nerve for many bread laborers, just as it did at the time of Gandhi's writing. While the development of agribusiness and other farming methods have changed the landscape considerably, the basic insights of Gandhi on this topic remain valid.

The Healing Value of Ordinary Labor

In the economic systems of developed countries, the opportunity to see the healing value of ordinary labor can easily be lost. In the global movement from an agrarian society to an industrial, and now to a post-industrial one, stories of individuals making a great deal of money or inheriting a fortune have become commonplace, although only a small fraction of the population achieves this status, and this is balanced against growing numbers of people living in extreme poverty. The urge for financial wealth is a daily cultural experience from the ticking Dow-Jones updates to the current lottery jackpot; all around us the craving for immediate gain is encouraged. In contrast, the value and true dignity of manual labor gets little attention.

The discipline of work has benefits well beyond the obvious material ones. William J. Wilson, professor of psychology at the University of Chicago, noted in a symposium at Cornell University in 1993 that, "Work is a critical organizing principle for the individual, the family, and even the neighborhood. The discipline of regular hours in and out of home has its impact on individual esteem and human development, including child development."

Gandhi believed in the discipline of work. He came to appreciate the value of everyone in the farm community sharing in the workload. He encouraged workers in factories to participate fully in the work of the mill and its organization. Likewise, he believed that to have a part in bread labor was also to have a part in wealth.

On the issue of wealth without work, Gandhi was able to draw on many personal experiences. He knew the poverty of workers and families in both South Africa and India. The indentured Indian workers in South Africa were paid a pittance. After their indentured period, they still struggled to make ends meet. In India, the situation of millions of Indians on family farms was equally as bad, if not worse. The land allotted to each family was not sufficiently fertile or large enough to produce enough to feed themselves. Gandhi's close friend, Jawaharlal Nehru, later to become the first prime minister of independent India, wrote that under British rule in the 19th century:

> The little land that each peasant household had was too small to support them decently. Poverty and semi starvation always faced them at the best of times. And often enough, the times were far from good. They were at the mercy of the seasons, the elements, and the monsoons. And famines came, and terrible diseases spread and carried off millions. They went to the *bania*, the village moneylenders, and borrowed money, and their debts grew bigger and bigger, and all hope and all possibility of payment passed, and life became a burden too heavy to be borne. Such became the condition of the vast majority of the population.

It was into this society that Gandhi spread the message of labor's worth by encouraging every home to have a simple, portable spinning wheel to use at least thirty minutes each day. He called this movement *charka* (hand spinning), and linked its benefits to a nonviolent lifestyle and the unification of India. Furthermore, it built upon the previous cultural experience of weaving. From Nehru's perspective, Gandhi gave hope to the poverty stricken people in the Indian villages and a sense of national identity, which had decayed under British rule.

Of course, spending time each day in some productive work had an economic dimension as well. Although the financial reward that villagers could realize was minute, it did supplement their meager income, occupied some of their time, and began to give back some of their cultural heritage. Yet, for Gandhi and eventually for the majority of India, it also came to have a political context by allowing families to bypass the purchase of foreign clothing and spin their own garments, known as *khadi* (homespun, hand woven cloth). Wearing khadi represented a desire for independence from colonialism. Eventually charka extended to city dwellers and virtually each of the seven hundred thousand villages of India.

A cartoonist from Germany captured the notion of Gandhi inspiring the whole country of India to spin (page xxvii). He framed it as Gandhi sitting in the lions' den, an appropriate image since he often found himself in hostile settings. As Daniel the Prophet was unafraid to speak the truth to King Balthazar, to share the bad news about the fall of his kingdom, so Gandhi was never afraid to speak truth to power. Like the prophet of old, Gandhi was sometimes an unwelcome guest when he criticized society. Daniel, whose insistence on prayer to his God landed him in the lions' pit, was spared any bodily harm. Likewise, Gandhi was viewed by some of the powerful leaders of his time as having simplistic solutions to complex problems. Like Daniel, he had a vital, active faith in God, nurtured by daily prayer. For Gandhi, religion was a constant. In the cartoon with all the hungry lions looking on, Gandhi sits peacefully spinning.

Gandhi's own experiments with truth brought him ever closer to simple living. If Gandhi visited the United States today and was asked what he would suggest to an ordinary citizen on the subject of wealth without work, we can surmise that he would echo his advice to Indian villagers - do something with your hands on a daily basis. He might recommend engaging in useful manual labor, something of value like composting, cooking, cleaning, gardening, or recycling- work on which to anchor moral development, yet give time for reflection.

To begin countering the social sin of wealth without work, he would likely focus on the importance of bread labor as well as volunteering. Additionally, in light of Gandhi's efforts to support striking mill workers, he would likely encourage the United States to bring into balance the ratio between capital and labor, between the salaries of white-collar and blue-collar workers, and an end to "golden parachutes," which he would surely view as morally offensive.

> "An infallible test of civilization is that a man claiming to be civilized should be an intelligent toiler, that he should understand the dignity of labor, and that his work should be such as to advance the interests of the community to which he belongs." —Gandhi

Gandhiji's Ten Commandments; 1928. Copyright: Vithalbhal Jhavert/Gandhi Server—KW: Mahatma Gandhi

GANDHIJI'S TEN COMMANDMENTS

"PERSONALLY, I WOULDN'T MAKE MUCH HEADWAY WITH 'EM IN MY BUSINESS. THEY ARE TOO IMPRACTICAL FOR MODERN CONDITIONS. BUT, OH BOY! WHAT A CLEAN-UP I COULD MAKE IF I HAD THE CONFIDENCE OF MILLIONS OF PEOPLE, THE WAY HE HAS!"

"THEY'RE ALL RIGHT FOR PLANKS IN A PLATFORM BUT NOT FOR PRACTICAL, EVERY DAY POLITICAL USE."

GANDHI'S PERSONAL TEN COMMANDMENTS FOR HIS OWN GUIDANCE—

1. Truth.
2. Love.
3. Chastity.
4. Restraint of the Appetites.
5. Possession only of essentials
6. One's Bread must be earned by the Sweat of one's brow.
7. Man's duty is to serve his neighbor
8. Equality of Mankind.
9. Equality of all the Great Faiths of the World.
10. Fearlessness

A caricature in a British journal in 1928 shows the reactions of a businessman and a politician to the standards Gandhi had set for their personal conduct. To these hard-boiled characters, Gandhi was an impractical idealist, a view popular in the ruling circles in Britain. Writing in *Young India* the same year, Gandhi declared that his creed was nonviolent "under all circumstances." He explained: "My method is conversion, not coercion. It is self-suffering, not the suffering of the tyrant. I know that method to be infallible." (1928)

Two

Pleasure Without Conscience

"It is good enough to talk of God whilst we are sitting here after a nice breakfast and looking forward to a nicer luncheon, but how am I to talk of God to the millions who have to go without two meals a day? To them, God can only appear as bread and butter."—Gandhi

Buddhist monk Thich Nhat Hanh, who was twenty-one when Gandhi was assassinated, was originally impressed with Gandhi not because of his theory or insight, but because of his success. Hanh said he later realized that success should not be the deepest type of influence. Gandhi would have agreed that the value of an action does not depend on whether or not it is successful.

A sense of mindfulness has been a hallmark of the Buddhist monk's subsequent teaching on cultivating awareness of everything that we eat, the care we give to that process, and our consumption of other products - themes that find resonance in Gandhi's life, going back to his student days. Reflecting on greed and the ethics of overconsumption, Hanh echoes Gandhi in teaching that they cause destruction and exploitation. In a 1988 interview Hahn declared, "Practicing mindfulness in the act of consuming is the basic act of social justice."

★★★

    Gandhi did not take much pleasure in material things, and he disciplined himself and continually moved towards greater asceticism. After establishing the Phoenix Settlement at the age of thirty-five, he began to seriously curtail his own sensory desires. He loved to eat, but gradually assumed a more bland diet within his vegetarian range. Gandhi's discipline about food consumption and proper eating habits testified to his self-restraint. Except for occasional meat served to Muslim members, the ashram diet was vegetarian. Gandhi came to believe that learning to control one's eating was the secret of harnessing the other senses. He wrote that a person "who has not mastered his palate cannot master the carnal desire. It is very difficult, I know, to master the palate. But mastery of the palate means automatic mastery of the other senses."

    Another component of Gandhi's lifestyle was his daily routine of exercise. He walked briskly each day, usually in the morning; companions often struggled to keep up with his pace. When engaged in his law practice in South Africa, Gandhi had often walked several hours to work and returning home.

    Within two years of founding the Phoenix Settlement, Gandhi took upon himself a vow of poverty, sharing most of the income from his then lucrative law practice with the emerging civil rights movement. He observed his duty of providing for the basic needs of his own family, but he came to see his obligations in a much wider perspective, both financially and emotionally. Being severe with himself, he was also severe with his sons. At times, he went out of his way to give other young men more attention and support than he gave to his own sons, much to their dismay and regret.

    During his time as an ambulance corps member during the 1906 Zulu Rebellion, Gandhi had significant time for reflection. The Zulu Rebellion was more of a police action than a war; nonetheless, Gandhi mobilized a group of Indians to form an ambulance corps under British auspices, just as he had previously done in the Second Boer War. The Zulu Rebellion was a one-sided affair that sickened Gandhi with its cruel slaughter of the tribesmen. He and his small group of fellow Indian noncombatants tended wounded Zulus—a task no Europeans were willing to perform. The violence, intensity and drudgery of the work led Gandhi to think more and more about how he wanted to focus his energy for the rest of his life. The idea of satyagraha began to crystallize in his mind and he came to the conclusion that in order to commit himself fully to public service he would have to forego the pleasures of food, sex and a comfortable lifestyle while refraining from hatred, anger and distractions.

Celibacy, in addition to cultivating inner strength, would also address the issue for Gandhi that after his four sons were born he did not wish to father other children. Gandhi began thinking about a *Brahmacharya* (personal vow of celibacy, asceticism). With the agreement of his wife, he decided that celibacy was necessary for his activist life as well as a way to practice birth control and model population control for others. This decision changed their relationship, resulting in what Gandhi perceived to be a deeper friendship. Kasturba was supportive of his civil movements—she could still be critical of him and angry with some of his demands—but she was proud of his work, and eventually led other women in social protests that harmonized with Gandhi's radical efforts. They took care of each other when one was sick, and Kasturba was by his side during several of Gandhi's prolonged fasts.

Gandhi found brachmacharya helpful to his own spiritual progress, and he encouraged others to follow suit. In the first decades of his self-imposed celibacy he encouraged married couples in his ashram to refrain from sexual activity while they were part of the community. He encouraged all married couples to pledge themselves to celibacy after their first child, although he later moderated his opinion on this issue. His willingness to reconsider his position occurred in part because Charles Andrews, his Anglican friend and biographer, questioned his wisdom on the subject.

Fifteen years after his vow, Gandhi explored the idea of celibacy in greater depth as he wrote about God and ethics while incarcerated in India's Yeravda prison. Ten years later, back in the same prison, Gandhi clarified those thoughts and published a small book on the subject of ethical perspectives, which included the need to discipline oneself by fasting and abstaining from sex except for the purpose of procreation. At this point he considered any other use of sex as a sin that offended both God and humanity. In prison, Gandhi reread the *Bhagavad-Gita;* Fischer writes that Gandhi considered one of the central teachings of the Hindu scripture to be: "Hold alike pleasure and pain, gain and loss, victory and defeat, and gird up thy loins for the fight; so doing thou shall not incur sin."

Although Gandhi had experienced intimacy at a very young age, he encouraged his sons and community members to abstain from sexual activity until they were older. An example of his sensitivity to the issue was a severe reprimand he gave his second son, Manilal, when he was eighteen, for kissing another young member of the ashram.

★★★

Gandhi had a very strong belief in God. His foundation principle was that God is truth and that as human beings we should exercise truth in thought, speech, and action. With these convictions, it is easy to see how Gandhi would have accepted, as a social sin, pleasure without conscience. Gandhi took pleasure in community, not in material things. In his ashrams he laid down strict rules for inclusion. Smoking, drinking, and sexual activity were not permitted. Despite these restrictions, the communities continued to grow, with members coming from several different religious backgrounds including Hindus, Muslims, Christians, and Parsi. In his first ashram in India, Sabarmati, the population of the community fluctuated from thirty at the beginning to over two hundred at its peak. Gandhi always seemed to attract disciples.

Gandhi became increasingly sensitive to any lack of spiritual awareness in individuals or society as he personally moved toward greater asceticism. As his personal discipline became more pronounced, the materialism and greed he sensed in Western culture became more acute. He was still not averse to criticizing fellow Indians over matters of lifestyle or personal hygiene. However, he found the moral values in village life, especially in India, to be far more profound and meaningful than those he observed in England and other Western societies.

Fasting

One of Gandhi's most effective "weapons" in his nonviolent movements was his ability to fast and to use his fasting as a platform for satyagraha. His willingness to fast became legendary, at times as a personal discipline, because of individual or group failings in moral matters, as a means of discernment for particular actions, or in an effort to curtail violence or social injustice. When he was unsure or unclear of what direction to take, he would fast. When circumstances arose that no longer allowed for rational discourse, he would fast. When relationships between individuals and groups became so frayed that violence was occurring or seen as latent, he would fast. When he reached a brick wall, when he was unsure of how to cope with various impediments, he turned to the discipline of fasting. The ability to fast was a powerful tool in Gandhi's moral life, and he used it again and again, often with maximum impact and positive results.

Twice he made the decision that social issues were so critical that he entered prolonged fasts, to the point of sacrificing his life. Once his motivation was to change the treatment and political representation of Untouchables; the other was an attempt to bring peace between Hindus and Muslims at a time of great tension and violence, for which he fasted for twenty-one days in an effort to move the country in the direction of harmony.

The response from those affected by Gandhi's fasts was spiritual, not because they were feeling forced to accept another's religious views or specific culture, but because people responded to Gandhi's *soul force* — his willingness to suffer for a cause that forced them to think about their own relationships. That is what Gandhi was about - relationships. For example, he chose to do his three-week fast in the home of a Muslim friend. When he fasted in a public way, the entire country paid attention, sometimes holding their collective breaths that he might not die in the effort. The British authorities also had serious concerns about their own public image, should Gandhi die in prison while fasting.

★★★

Fasting was a part of Catholic tradition during my youth. The concept of a fast before a feast remains in my psyche and provides special meaning for holy days and holidays. Fasting on certain days of the year and choosing voluntary periods of fasting has been helpful for many seeking balance in their lives. While never experiencing the kind of extended fasting that Gandhi did, it was a measure of discipline that helped me prepare for arrest at the S.O.A. and subsequent incarceration, and I know that many of my fellow protesters also found it helpful.

Prison Insights

A few observations from my prison experience tie in with the idea of pleasure without conscience as a social sin. At Canaan Federal Prison Camp, the food provided for the inmates was very adequate, although much of it came from a great distance. Inmates were aware that the dates stamped on processed-food packages were often past expiration, making them ineligible for the shelves of American grocery stores. How much better, I thought, to grow some of the food on the abundant acreage of the prison grounds by the inmates themselves. Sites could be created for composting fruit and vegetable leftovers. This, in turn, would reduce trash, while the compost would enrich the soil for fertile gardening. For many inmates coming from city settings, the chance to experience the cycles of nature could be educational, as well as helpful in developing job-training skills. The useful labor would come as a welcome relief from some of the "make-work" projects to which many prisoners are assigned, such as cutting the grass when it is not needed.

Although a larger, medium-security federal prison occupies adjacent land, there is considerable open space on the prison camp campus, including an old apple orchard that could be brought back into production. These untapped land resources, together with an inmate labor pool of many willing workers, who would have welcomed the opportunity to participate in providing for the common good, painted a sad picture of wasted potential.

Except for the limited time allowed to eat each meal, I had no complaints about the quality or quantity of the food. My concerns had to do with the amount of waste I was witnessing. This, together with the poor usage of available land, conflicted with my environmental consciousness, developed over recent years by weekly recycling, returning bottles, and backyard gardening with a compost pile nearby. None of this was evident at the prison, where a large amount of food was thrown away on a daily basis.

This waste disturbed many inmates. I heard one prisoner, a former military sergeant, say to a food-service worker who was preparing to throw unused loaves of bread from the meal into the large garbage pail, "How about giving it to a local food pantry?" There was no acknowledgement or reply! The bread was cast away, as were several unused pans of cooked lasagna. Stories of this kind of waste came to me from other inmates, even as I was observing the throwaway mentality on a regular basis.

Because of these concerns, I sent a formal suggestion to the prison-camp administrator regarding composting and recycling. She sent me a prompt response, but no changes ensued. I then sent a letter to *The Post-Standard* in Syracuse, which was published under the heading: "First Impressions of Federal Prison: What a Waste":

> …On both a micro and macro level, however, the waste within the system is appalling. In this satellite camp alone, the amount of food thrown away on a daily basis would provide individuals or families at the Samaritan Center or other local places like Unity Kitchen with ample nutrition for a week. Some of it comes from the inmates' taking more food than they can eat or choose to eat at one sitting; some comes from a food service that throws away many of the leftovers.
>
> There is no recycling in this facility—no effort to separate bottles, cans, or small cardboard containers from the trash; no garden; no effort to conserve water; none of the environment-friendly things that good stewardship invites and encourages.

A copy of the article circulated around the prison camp, and was even put up on a Corrections list serve. While many of the inmates and even some of the corrections officers told me they appreciated my efforts, the administration did not. They called me in for a conference, where I appealed to my First Amendment right to freedom of speech. That basically ended the discussion, with a strict warning about future correspondence without authorization.

My work assignment at the prison was landscaping, a job that I requested because I wanted to work outside as well as explore the potential for alternative use of the land. When I asked the landscape supervisor about the possibility of developing a compost pile for the facility, he was open to the idea. I brought him materials on the subject that my younger sister and another friend had sent me.

Some inmates at our satellite camp had previously been at a prison in Duluth, Minnesota where an efficient indoor vermicompost (worm compost) system is in place. Two of these inmates helped me prepare a similar design that I presented to the landscape supervisor. After we discussed some of the elements in a good system that would develop the composted "black gold," the supervisor mentioned the carbon-nitrogen ratio needed for proper balance. It was reason for hope, not only because of his interest but also his knowledge about composting. He told me that he thought we could get one started shortly, in an outdoor location. The food staff inmates and their supervisor also seemed ready to cooperate.

After considering the matter, however, my supervisor indicated that he wanted to get permission for the project from a superior in the chain of command. The line involved at least four people, up to the warden. He requested that I draft a letter to his immediate supervisor, which I did. The letter was sent, but a response never came. Inmates who were interested in the composting possibility were not surprised by the inaction. It was similar to the lack of attention given to almost every suggestion initiated by the inmates.

★★★

For over twenty-five years, our family has had a compost bin in our backyard. On a regular basis, even in the winter months, we set aside all kinds of organic materials: vegetable trimmings, fruit peelings, eggshells and coffee grounds. In the spring I shovel out the fine topsoil to spread on our vegetable gardens and flowerpots. What has been added after my prison experience is a vermicomposting system, a box of wriggly red worms, in our cellar. With a little work, a portion of our garbage gets eaten, and black gold compost and compost tea for our plants and garden soil is our reward for the easy effort.

Our younger daughter tells a story about a grammar-school adventure. When her teacher asked for parent volunteers to take willing class members to interesting places, I volunteered to explain composting. She assumed it would be an unpopular choice, but a carload of third graders came to our backyard where I explained the workings of a compost pile. To this day, she reminds me of that experience, laughingly mentioning that, at the conclusion of my presentation, I gave each of them an apple. I probably encouraged them to throw the core in the compost pile. That way, nothing went to waste. Would that this opportunity were available in prison settings!

Chavez's Witness

Cesar Chavez, a student of Gandhi's nonviolent approach, is an excellent example of a person who sacrificed his own comfort for an ideal and a cause. Chavez participated in his first field strike in 1940, when he was thirteen years old and picking grapes in California. He watched as his father organized a hundred fellow workers and approached the manager with the group's demands: minimum wage of fifty cents an hour, overtime after eight hours in the field, no child labor, and separate toilets for women and men. His father was accused of being a communist and the owner brought in Mexican workers and replaced the "discontented" strikers.

That lesson stayed with young Chavez. When he returned to the agricultural fields after completing military service, at the age of twenty-four, he met Fred Ross of the Community Services Organization who began to teach him organizing techniques. Ross and Chavez embarked on a voter-registration drive for Mexican-Americans. Chavez patiently worked on this project, teaching basic reading and writing skills, citizenship, and length-of-residency requirements, which helped prepare the workers to vote.

Ross later became one of the main organizers for Saul Alinsky's Industrial Area Foundation. It was in this role that he was chosen as the field director of the Community Action Training Center—a pilot project in Lyndon Johnson's War on Poverty. This program, set up by the Syracuse University School of Social Work, trained community organizers.

★★★

As a participant in this program, I first met Chavez in 1965, when Ross introduced us. The community project that Ross was directing included the development of eight organizations in various city neighborhoods in Syracuse. After a few short months, residents were already advocating for themselves by bringing their considerable concerns and complaints to places like the Housing Authority and local government agencies. In theory, the rationale for the project made considerable sense. In practice, once it began to be implemented, it rubbed some people the wrong way. Organizing citizens from poor neighborhoods to challenge city hall and other government entities was not acceptable to some political leaders and Syracuse University alumni, who put pressure on the university, which in turn backed away from its initial commitment. As a result, the Community Action Training Center lasted barely a year.

Fortunately, the techniques that Ross taught Chavez in community organizing were not subject to governmental veto. Yet it was not simply these techniques that allowed Chavez to establish the United Farm Workers (UFW) union. Chavez was also dedicated to the principles and witness of Gandhi, from whom he drew great inspiration.

Chavez, like Gandhi, appreciated fasting as a tactic. It had great spiritual value for both men, since it connected prayer and their own self-discipline. During the historic 1968 grape boycott Chavez fasted for twenty-five days as an incentive for workers to remain nonviolent. His fast ended with Senator Robert Kennedy at his side. In July 1988, Chavez undertook his longest fast, thirty-six days, to raise public awareness of pesticide use. His goal was to ban the five most deadly pesticides that were poisoning farm workers and community water supplies. The fast succeeded in raising public awareness of this issue. Asked about its effect, Chavez replied, "It did a lot. The fast is a great communicator. Like Gandhi, because we don't have the economic or political force, we have to appeal to the moral force, and the boycott is the best instrument. Gandhi said that the boycotts were the most near-perfect instrument for social change."

Each fast for Chavez was an opportunity to bring about a change of heart for those in a position of authority who could do something to change negative conditions but do nothing. His leadership in the UFW's successful grape boycott conveyed his belief in the power of boycotts and the need for moral awareness and personal action by consumers. These convictions have since influenced community organizers in various cultures on critical issues around the world.

Chavez gives us an example of action on a macro-level as well. Despite some improvements in conditions since his father's time, the UFW faced a considerable challenge in its original organizing effort. The National Labor Relations Act (NRLA), passed in 1935, placed a spotlight on labor and workers' rights. The major problem Chavez encountered in organizing farm workers had to do with one of the few exception in the NLRA—agriculture. Some of the language of the legislation, known as the Wagner Act, was drawn from Catholic social teachings that defend the just wage, the right of workers to organize, and the need for limited state intervention to insure these rights. It was through Chavez's work and others involved in the national boycotts on lettuce and grapes that agricultural workers were eventually included under this federal labor protection.

Gandhi made his appeal to the conscience of caring individuals saying, "Conscience is the ripe fruit of strictest discipline...The introduction of conscience into our public life is welcome if it has taught a few of us to stand up for human dignity and rights in the face of the heaviest odds." This sentiment fits both Chavez's and Gandhi's efforts in several ways. Chavez gave a face to some of the least-powerful people in the country—migrant farm workers, as Gandhi had challenged the caste system and advocated for Untouchables. Like his spiritual mentor, Chavez always carried out his actions in a nonviolent manner, and insisted upon this approach for those who wished to join in his efforts. There were other parallels between the two men. They both accepted fasting as a self-disciplined way to share their concerns. These efforts were often unpopular, yet both of them received recognition and respect.

Chavez helped bring home to Americans a truth that is easily missed in a culture where food is usually bought in supermarkets. From the lettuce we eat in our salads to table grapes and grapes turned into fine California wines, culinary delights on our dinner tables, which often come from hundreds or thousands of miles away, might well have been grown and harvested under dangerous conditions by low paid farm workers.

Chavez also helped focus attention on Gandhi's nonviolence by modeling it. Chavez believed that Gandhi's witness for nonviolence went beyond his immediate environment; it was a message for the whole world. Leading the way, Gandhi showed how it could work. It was an inspiration for Chavez, who once said that the book that had influenced him most was Gandhi's *The Story of My Experiments with Truth*.

Gandhi's Reflections

Gandhi's autobiography, begun at age fifty-six, focused on his experiments with honesty. As Erik Erikson points out in his psychological study, *Gandhi's Truth*, the autobiography was not originally a book, but rather a series of articles in his weekly journal: "It took the Mahatma years to write the installments which, at the end, became a book that was no book, and which yet, maybe for that reason, impressed millions of readers who could 'take' a chapter at a time, as one takes a sermon and a lesson at a time."

In his personal writings Gandhi revealed the roots of the abstemious lifestyle exercised by himself and his followers, especially concerning sexual mores. He entered into a family-arranged marriage when he and his bride Kastur were both thirteen. Based partly on his own experience, Gandhi worked passionately to eradicate the tradition of child marriage in India. When women were widowed, even as children or teenagers, they were not allowed to remarry. (Even today, this is an issue for widows in India.) What disturbed Gandhi most was the abuse of women, which he perceived to be a result of this Hindu tradition, and it was women who were the most grateful for his work on this issue.

Gandhi's opposition to child marriage also hints at an explanation for his advocacy of celibacy. Understandably, he knew very little of what such a union implied when he was wed. There were long periods away from his family, leaving his wife to care for their first child, Harilal who was born when Gandhi was seventeen. As a youth, Harilal spent limited time with his father and later blamed him for not caring for him. Harilel married at seventeen and also fathered four children, but after his wife died in the devastating influenza epidemic of 1918 his life disintegrated and he became an alcoholic. Harilal turned against his father, denouncing him in various public ways. Their son's rejection was a crushing blow to his parents, especially Kasturba who was shamed by Harilal's alcoholic behavior. Gandhi long recognized his own failure as a father and as a spouse in the early years of marriage, admitting that he himself was growing up at the same time as his first son.

★★★

The political cartoon (page 15) portraying Gandhi's Ten Commandments appeared in 1928. The artist depicts aspects of Gandhi's philosophy that were seen as unrealistic by the "fat cats" of his day. These same principles are a challenge to many of us today, and they help us recognize the disciplined way that Gandhi dealt with himself, his family, and those who sought to join in his various movements. The rules that emerged in his ashrams seem harsh from the vantage point of modern/postmodern promiscuous Western culture, but they seemed to resonate within the stricter settings of ashrams and the larger Hindu and Islamic religious traditions. Yet always there was great love and laughter in these communities. Gandhi did not take himself so seriously that he was unable to change his mind, or admit his inconsistencies, or to enjoy laughter, even at his own expense. He loved children and was playful around them, especially after his own sons had grown into adulthood.

The imperative of awareness and the need for personal action that was demonstrated by Gandhi and Chavez is relevant to many dimensions of American culture today, where citizens may experience frustration as they observe themselves as bystanders and collaborators in decisions with which they disagree but find themselves as powerless to address. This frustration extends from major government decisions, like preemptive war, to local ordinances regarding trash collection or environmental concerns like storm water drainage.

The term community organizer was never associated with Gandhi, yet that was the role that he often played. He looked for opportunities to challenge unjust laws and actions in both South Africa and India. His decisions were not about his own actions as much as they were about motivating and inspiring others to participate. What might Gandhi say to American citizens if he were to visit the United States today? In the same teasing way that he explained many of his lessons to potential followers, he would ask about habits and desires. In this way, he would lead us to reflect on our own self-discipline, how our present lifestyle might match up with the list of priorities that the cartoonist identified. While his manner would be gentle with a touch of humor, his message would not be subtle. Work on your own self-disciple to begin matching up with your own ideals. Practice sexual restraint, even abstinence, until a mature decision about entering into a lifelong commitment can be made. Respect the teaching of your own religion or religious background. If much of America considers itself a Christian nation, Gandhi might question why many of those claiming to be Christians do not live according to the teachings of Christ. He did ask those questions to Christian missionaries on more than one occasion. His style of communication was both blunt and non-aggressive, which was how Gandhi worked with individuals. It was his way of recruiting people to consider satyagraha in their own lives.

> "Happiness, the goal to which we are all striving, is reached by endeavoring to make the lives of others happy, and if by renouncing the luxuries of life we can lighten the burden of others…surely the simplification of our wants is a thing greatly to be desired." —Gandhi

The Congress Working Committee met in 1930 and decided on civil disobedience to promote the objective of genuine Indian self-rule. What shape would it take? After a two-month period of reflection, Gandhi indicated that it would be resistance to the salt tax. Writing in *Young India*, his English weekly, he asked how, outside of taxing water, could any tax be so devastating to "the starving millions, the maimed, and utterly helpless. This tax constitutes, therefore, the most inhuman poll tax the ingenuity of man can devise." Gandhi's decision aroused worldwide interest, as this American cartoon shows. (1930)

Three

Commerce Without Morality

"Herein is a practical lesson for any nation or individual. The measure of a nation's or individual's self-sacrifice must ever be the measure of their growth." —Gandhi

One follower of Gandhi's philosophy and spirituality was A.T. Ariyaratne, a Sri Lankan Buddhist, who focused his energy on the collective aspects of work and its interface with the international economic system. Ariyaratne went to India to study social movements, especially the *Bhoodan-Gramdan* (land-gift) campaign, in which land donations from rich to poor rendered four million acres of land available for food production. While the land gift campaign came as a result of Vinobe Bhave's work after Gandhi's death, its achievement is considered to be one of the great legacies of Gandhi.

In a 1984 interview, Ariyaratne discussed the worsening conditions for the poor in Sri Lanka, connecting its poverty to "the international economy ...controlled by so few people." While those with power generally reside in affluent nations, the people who actually produce most of the world's food and labor-intensive products live primarily in poorer countries. Ariyaratne observed that the manufacturing of processed food in Sri Lanka cost more than the food itself, with all the added chemicals that are fused in the process.

Ariyaratne did not advocate for international trade. Like Gandhi, he observed the injustice it produced by crippling the income of small farmers in his own country and believed that it was driven by the greed of rich people in rich countries. When Sri Lanka sells its goods, the money received is often spent to buy unnecessary goods—a process fostered by advertising. Ariyaratne saw this as a vicious cycle, with poor countries experiencing the greatest damage. He agreed with activists and community organizers in developing countries, including many in Central and South America, who are opposed to regional free-trade agreements. The abundance of produce going into Latin America from first-world countries diminishes its own farmers' profit margin. This system also ensures that food on many tables comes from long distances.

The rules set up by the General Agreement on Tariffs and Trade (GATT) do not favor the small farmer in developing countries. GATT, established in 1947 after the Bretton Woods conference that set international monetary policy, created rules that were optional for nearly half a century. However, with the creation of the World Trade Organization in 1995, GATT lost its voluntary nature.

Gandhi clearly did not support free trade. An economic principle that appealed to him can be found in the Hindu word *swadeshi*, (adherence to, or use of, what was made in or belongs to one's own country). For Gandhi, swadeshi was a religious idea that extended to politics and economics. He blamed much of the deep poverty in India on the abandonment of this principle and held Britain responsible for forcing trade upon India. Gandhi had long and arduous discussions about this concept with Andrews, who said of Gandhi, "In swadeshi, he finds a principle which explains his relationship to Christianity and other religions. There is to him a religious patriotism, as well as a patriotism of national status."

Gandhi told a story to illustrate his point on the importance of attending to local concerns: if a barber in a particular location was not very adept at his profession, Gandhi thought it would be better for the community to use his services rather than go to a barber in another area. Gandhi suggested helping the local barber improve his skills through training and continual encouragement. Such a culture of local support within villages and small communities had been part of Gandhi's upbringing in Porbandar, a small state in western India. His mother's guidance helped him understand that if each person cares for and attends to his or her local community, the rest of the world will take care of itself.

Gandhi's appreciation for the deep spiritual values in Indian culture can be seen in his correspondence with Leo Tolstoy in 1909, when Gandhi returned to England to advocate against restrictions on the Indian population in South Africa. Yogesh Chadha, in his biography *Gandhi, A Life* identified a profound change in Gandhi's thinking at this time. It came partly from his reading of Tolstoy and Henry David Thoreau, but also from his disillusionment with Western civilization. The influence of another author, G.K. Chesterton, helped Gandhi identify some of the evils that arose from the British occupation of India. Earlier, Gandhi had generally praised the British rule of law and government. Now began the evolution of his thinking on the importance of India's need to move toward self-rule. Some of these ideas came from Indian writers, including the poet Rabindranath Tagore, and some came from the meaningful dialogues he had with young Indians in London.

Indian Home Rule

After a three-month visit to London in 1909, Gandhi felt frustrated on his homeward voyage to South Africa, just as he had felt after his visit two years earlier. This time, his best efforts on behalf of blocking the Black Act had failed. Aboard the ship Gandhi wrote his thoughts about home rule for India, completing a thirty thousand-word document called *Hind Swaraj* in less than a week. *Hind Swaraj* not only criticized British colonial rule, but also pointedly addressed the greed that Gandhi had observed on his trip and that he believed was spreading in the West. Even though, at this point in his life, he was engaged in the struggles of Indians in South Africa, his broader focus was on home rule in India.

Hind Swaraj was first published in weekly installments in *Indian Opinion*; the manuscript later became his first book. In the text, Gandhi used a Socratic format, where a reader poses a question and the editor responds. *Hind Swaraj* revealed Gandhi's social reasoning on how India should proceed in order to obtain independence from the British. He asserted that the iron hand of Britain had to be challenged. Moreover, the primary catalyst would be for Indians themselves to exercise self-control that equated to self-rule. *Swaraj* (independence, personal spiritual renewal) became one of Gandhi's central beliefs.

In response to the idea that England occupied India and held it by the sword, Gandhi wrote:

> The sword is entirely useless for holding India...We like their commerce; they please us by their subtle methods and get what they want from us...We further strengthen their hold by quarreling among ourselves...India is being ground down not under the British heel but under that of modern civilization.

Hind Swaraj caused strong reaction in India, both positive and negative. Although Gandhi would remain in South Africa for five more years, this publication and the satyagraha campaigns in

South Africa caught the attention of many Indian politicians and intellectuals long before his return home.

Gandhi returned to India at the beginning of World War I. Once established in a new ashram, he began his campaign encouraging use of the spinning wheel. Spinning allowed individuals from all social classes to work with their hands in productive labor. Gandhi saw dignity and self-confidence emerging for those who embraced his challenge of even a half-hour of spinning labor each day. For him, the wheel was a symbol of simplicity and economic freedom—a symbol of peace. For Gandhi, it was not globalization, but idleness, whether enforced or voluntary, that led to human tragedy. Given his conviction, inspiring inhabitants of an entire village to work with their hands helped address this national malady. To accomplish this goal, his organizational tool, beyond person-to-person contact, was the printing press. It helped inform his constituents of violations of basic human rights and encouraged them to engage in positive, personal action.

Nicaraguan Model

In the early 1980s I was a member of several Witness for Peace delegations to Nicaragua. We observed the country in the aftermath of the 1979 revolution, which deposed the dictator, Anastasio Somoza. The Somoza family had controlled Nicaragua for forty-four years. On these trips our groups noticed great societal changes occurring soon after the Sandinista government took over. In many ways, the Sandinistas were walking the delicate road between socialism and capitalism, with considerable initial success. With assistance from local banks, farm cooperatives were widely established. Billboards no longer advertised commercial products, but instead, announced basic, health-related information. Some of the young people who formerly loitered on the streets returned to school, and literacy rates among youth gradually rose to over eighty percent. Homes were set up to support prostitutes, encouraging them to embrace a different lifestyle and become respected citizens. A Maryknoll priest became the Secretary of State. The poet laureate of Nicaragua, Ernesto Cardenal, also a priest, became the Minister of Culture.

Many American corporations were still doing business in Nicaragua, but their connections, prestige, and profile were diminishing. The United States government under President Reagan was unhappy with Sandinista restraints on outside commercial interests and concerned that U.S. corporations would lose their strong fiscal positions in Nicaragua. Moreover, in the waning years of the Cold War, the American government wanted to eradicate any communist threat in the Western Hemisphere.

To address this problem, the United States needed to change the Sandinistas policies, or remove them from power. To that end, the U.S. military helped organize and arm an insurgent army based in neighboring Honduras. These soldiers, including former military personnel of the Somoza régime, became known as Contras. Nicaragua fell into to civil war and eventually the Contra's pressure on the country was too great for the people to sustain a progressive democracy. The political scene changed when the Sandinista president, Daniel Ortega, lost the 1989 election. Soon much of the capitalist economy was back in place, and wealth was still concentrated in a tiny percentage of the overall population.

★★★

Gandhi's focus on commerce and morality connects to my experience with two towns in Nicaragua. In the mid 1980's, our parish developed a sister-community relationship with a small village in the northwest corner of Nicaragua near Honduras, named Dulce Nombre de Jesus (Sweet Name of Jesus). The project later expanded to the nearby town of Villanueva. Through our contact with two Maryknoll sisters working there, the relationship has given us the opportunity to support their health-related programs with regular funding from our parish tithe. The focus of our efforts has been to help the community develop a network of volunteer health promoters. Over two hundred individuals, mostly women, come from outlying areas into Villanueva for monthly workshops. These trainings are held by a small, dedicated team of local health professionals who teach the volunteers to be health workers specializing in prevention, medical assistance, and herbal remedies. Some of the volunteers walk for many miles, leaving their homes very early in the morning, to attend training sessions. Youth programs providing social activities and health education have also been part of this project, Villanueva's health outreach programs have flourished over the past eighteen years. This has been just one small effort to assist a Central-American nation with difficult political and economic struggles.

After the devastating floods of Hurricane Mitch in 1998, ten St. Andrews parishioners visited Villanueva. Several of us worked daily alongside residents on construction of a thirty five-unit housing project that was made up of simple cinder block homes and latrines. There was no running water or electricity available for the new units, yet no funding was available from the Nicaraguan government. The large debt that Nicaragua owes to the International Monetary Fund (IMF) may be one reason the government does not have the resources to fund such projects.

Nicaragua, the second poorest country in the Western Hemisphere (after Haiti), needs more than shoestring support in order to improve its economy. Rather than continuing to make high interest payments on loans without ever touching the principal, developing countries such as Nicaragua could be forgiven a good portion of their debt to enable them to improve politically, economically, and socially. This letter to the editor was published in 1999:

> What a jubilee idea! Your editorial last Sunday, 'Forgive Debt,' endorsed a common sense plan that would ease the terrible economic burden currently hindering development in many Third-World countries.
>
> The situation for several African and Latin-American countries is akin to persons getting so far behind in credit card payments that they can never catch up with the interest debt, let alone the principal.
>
> The jubilee concept found in the Hebrew Law of Moses (Leviticus and Exodus) laid out the ideal that there needs to be a time when debilitating debts are forgiven. As we move toward a new millennium, the time is ripe, and the need is great. The Jubilee 2000 movement helps bring these ideas into focus.
>
> It is estimated that every child born in Nicaragua assumes a $2,000 debt to this fund—a cumulative one that can never be paid off under the present circumstances. Your editorial mentions three other countries experiencing the same hopeless struggle. Many of the poor in the world are in the same economic boat. Forgiveness of these debts would cause little more than a ripple in our economic picture.
>
> Yet, it would mean so much to the countries affected. The biblical roots of forgiveness are deep in the Hebrew Scripture, and Jesus made it a cornerstone of His teaching.
>
> President Clinton's proposal to forgive the debt of certain countries that are willing to spend the saved funds on health care, education, or vital basic needs makes economic and moral sense. Now is the time for the Congress to rise above partisan politics on this vote.

As your editorial stated, 'Congress has the opportunity in one act to determine how this country will be viewed through the prism of history.' That may be optimistic, but it is certainly a chance to make amends for some of our destructive foreign policies in the past. We do know that a jubilee train with this momentum doesn't come along very often.

Maritime Entanglements

Commercial interests among nations and continents have become so intricate that sorting out the moral responsibility when something goes wrong is difficult. However, the issues become more urgent when people are injured in the process. The following incident, which occurred in 2006, highlights the challenge of holding companies and countries liable. It involved a Greek-owned tanker, flying a Panamanian flag, which was leased by the British branch of a Swiss trading corporation with fiscal headquarters in the Netherlands. This is where this story begins.

The Greek tanker, leased by Trafigura, a global oil and metals trading company, arrived in Amsterdam in early July to unload two hundred and fifty tons of regular slops, which is the wash water from cleaning a ship's holds. According to a report in the *International Herald-Tribune*, the volume was actually about four hundred tons, much higher than anticipated, and the seeping fumes from the waste sickened some of the Dutch workers unloading it. "It was pitch black and had a heavy stench," said a spokesperson for the Amsterdam Port Services. "No one had ever seen similar waste."

The waste-processing company stopped unloading the sludge, ordered analysis, and informed the Amsterdam city authorities of the presence of hazardous waste. The sludge was found to have high levels of caustic soda, and hydrogen sulfide, which is a volatile compound that smells like rotten eggs. At high concentrations, hydrogen sulfide can no longer be smelled because it paralyzes the nervous system. It remained unclear where the waste originated. Trafigura refused to pay the fees for safe disposal, which would have cost as little as $300,000, despite revenues of twenty-eight billion the previous year.

Instead, Dutch authorities released the vessel, which sailed to Estonia. There it took on Russian oil products, which were delivered to Nigeria. The tanker then sailed for Ivory Coast, arriving in Abidjan on August 9th, a month after leaving Amsterdam. Trafigura then contracted with a local company named Tommy, which in turn hired more than a dozen tanker trucks into which the sludge was pumped. At night, the trucks pumped the toxic liquid across Abidjan into at least eighteen neighborhoods. Eight people died, dozens were hospitalized, and 85,000 residents sought medical attention. One man reported that the skin of his six-month-old son "bloomed with blisters, which burst into weeping sores all over his body," and that his entire family was suffering from headaches, nosebleeds, and stomach aches.

Who was held accountable? As imagined, there was a denial of responsibility from many of the countries involved. Initially, even though the pungent odor was affecting residents, the Ivorian government did not acknowledge what had happened. Left to the aggrieved citizens to force action, it took demonstrations from the local population to focus attention on government corruption and bring about an investigation. The resulting furor caused the prime minister of the Ivory Coast and his government to resign (although many were later reinstated). Six individuals from the Ivory Coast were jailed, along with two European Trafigura officials and a single Nigerian. Greenpeace filed criminal complaints against Trafigura, Amsterdam Port Services, and the Dutch environmental authorities. The Greenpeace expert in toxic waste explained, "The whole procedure was illegal: first, allowing the waste in, then pumping it back on board…and letting the ship leave without any licenses."

The involvement of seven countries in this single incident sheds light on the complexity of global commerce. The sludge-deposit tragedy highlights the underbelly of globalization. The end result of poor people literally being dumped upon brings into focus the social sin of commerce without morality. Since the creation of the World Bank and IMF, poor nations and indigenous people have had little opportunity to shape policies that protect their own resources and the living conditions of their people.

Effects on Indigenous Populations

The plight of indigenous people around the world received increased attention when Guatemalan Rigoberta Menchu received the Nobel Peace Prize in 1992. As Menchu and her fellow refugees were returning to their native country after ten years of exile, this letter to the editor was published in *The Post Standard:*

> In a long line of distinguished Nobel Prize recipients, Roberta Menchu, a thirty-three-year-old Guatemalan woman, received the honor on December 10. It came at a crucial point in her country's history, as refugees who fled from Guatemala prepared to return to their homeland after ten years of exile in Southern Mexico.
>
> As a native Mayan Indian, Menchu symbolizes the survival of indigenous people who have long been exploited. The suffering she witnessed by members of her own family, while extreme, reflects the lives of many of the indigenous native peoples and of the 87 percent of Guatemalans who live in poverty.
>
> As a young child, she migrated annually, with other members of her family, to plantations where peasants work picking products for export. Two of her brothers died on those plantations—one of malnutrition; the other of pesticide poisoning. She saw another brother publicly executed during the government's military forays in the highlands.
>
> In 1980, her father, Vincente Menchu, led a peaceful sit-in at the Spanish Embassy to publicize the massacres and land seizures. Along with thirty-eight others, he burned to death at that location in a fire set by the Guatemalan army.
>
> Later that same year, her mother was kidnapped and killed. Through all this tragedy, Menchu continued to organize native people until forced to flee for her life.
>
> The timely peace prize will focus international attention on the efforts of native people to return to their

homeland with some sense of dignity and security. The life and spirit of this extraordinary woman, as well as the struggle of indigenous people for the healing of a nation, are found in her autobiography, *I, Rigoberta Menchu*.

Jeannette Armstrong, in the book *Paradigm Wars: Indigenous Peoples' Resistance to Globalization*, describes the way nation-states are continuously reconfiguring economic boundaries for the advantage of big business:

> This is causing a tidal flow of refugees from environmental and social disasters, compounded by disease and famine, as people are displaced in the rapidly expanding worldwide chaos. War itself becomes continuous as dispossession, privatization of lands, exploitation of resources, and a cheap labor force becomes the mission of 'peace keeping.' Finding new markets are the justification for the westernization of 'undeveloped' cultures.

Nevertheless, indigenous people throughout the world are engaged in organizing to assert their rights. After decades of discussion, the UN General Assembly passed the Declaration of the Rights of Indigenous Peoples in September 2007. Inexplicably, the United States was one of four countries that voted against the declaration, despite one hundred and twenty four countries approving it. The declaration brought a renewed focus to many documents that preceded or were promulgated simultaneously with the voyages of Columbus. The *Doctrine of Discovery* was a series of documents that gave Christian explorers the right to claim sovereignty over land they "discovered." They were based on Papal Bulls written by one eleventh century pope, Urban II, and two fifteenth century popes, Nicholas V and Alexander VI. Eventually, this doctrine was incorporated into laws in Europe and the United States.

Indigenous communities are now asking that this doctrine be reviewed and reconsidered. They recognize that it has been used as a basic argument for private property rights that often conflict with indigenous cultural mores of sustainable use and protection of the earth. Reexamining the *Doctrine of Discovery* helps place some of the treaties between governments and indigenous groups under a legal microscope. The Vatican claims that this doctrine was abrogated long ago; many from indigenous communities want a more formal apology, even though it would not change any present laws.

Within this context, coalitions of indigenous groups continue to make their voices heard, not only for past grievances, but also on the very serious current issue of global warming. On Earth Day 2008, Oren Lyons, chief of the Onondaga Nation and spokesperson for the Haudenosaunee (Iroquois) Alliance, addressed the Permanent Forum of Indigenous Issues at the UN. Lyons said that balance is the key to peace on earth, the health of the earth and the well being of all of its inhabitants. He recalled how in 1977, one hundred and forty six indigenous delegations traveled to Geneva to address the UN. These delegations warned of "the dire consequences of the reckless exploitation of the earth by industrial states." The following year an indigenous runner from Greenland informed the UN in New York that the ice was melting in the North. In 2000, Chief Lyons spoke on the same topic at the UN Millennium World Peace Summit of Religious and Spiritual Leaders:

> Every day that we do not address this issue as a global problem is another day of lost options until we reach the tipping point of the great natural systems that govern our lives on earth, the point of no return...We now must create a new paradigm, undertake a fundamental change of direction. We must change the values driving today's dominant economies. We must transform the values of commerce and commercialism to those of conservation, cooperation, and sharing. We must simplify our lives and renew our understanding of our relationship to the earth as the Mother of Life.

While the concept of private property is generally regarded as law in every country, many scholars and theologians recognize that there is a social mortgage attached to that right. Some indigenous communities see an entirely separate paradigm for property rights beyond discussions held in courts. This ideology embraces a spirituality that focuses on humans as trustees of the earth and considers how land use will affect seven future generations. Most indigenous cultures perceive a relationship to a great creative spirit, honored by many titles, which recognizes the land as a gift from the Creator and implies stewardship of all creation. This relationship connects human beings everywhere with animals and plants. In short, the belief is that God owns the land, and we, the tenants, must use it and share it wisely. The ongoing advocacy by indigenous peoples before environmental forums at the United Nations calls to mind Gandhi's emphasis on self-reliance, connection to the land, and respect for all life.

Liberation Theology

Liberation theology is an interpretation of the gospel as pro-social justice, with special concern for the poor. The term liberation theology was not in general use during Gandhi's time, but the spiritual and practical applications of this concept resonate with his thinking and actions, including his advocacy for the Untouchable population.

Theologians in Latin America introduced the concept of liberation theology in the late 1960's. It includes the concept of a preferential option for the poor. While this phrasing was new to many, the idea behind it was firmly rooted in the Hebrew and Christian scriptures and in both religious traditions. If God has a special concern for the poor, as these scriptures teach, then issues like war, the environment, distribution of resources, and taxation need to be considered from the perspective of those most affected by them. It is a theological approach from the bottom up, rather than control coming down from religious leaders or politicians. While the voices of disadvantaged people have traditionally been muted, liberation theology seeks to amplify them in a manner that will impact public policy.

In 1925, Gandhi stepped away from a formal political role and traveled throughout India encouraging use of the spinning wheel and collecting funds to move the country in the direction of self-rule. To help the poor and the outcasts in society, he taught, you must understand them. To understand them, one must work as they do. Thus, he encouraged everyone, rich and poor, politicians and peasants, to spin.

Like the subsequent development of liberation theology, Gandhi's vision of the spinning wheel movement was broad, including the liberation of women; "bringing them out from their seclusion," he said, "as nothing else has done…. It has given them a dignity and self-confidence which no university degree could give them." What could better describe liberation theology in Gandhian terms than his efforts with the spinning wheel?

March to the Sea

In a dramatic moment in India's movement toward independence, Gandhi, at age sixty-one, led a defining march to the sea to protest the British salt tax. The 1930 cartoon (page 34) published in the *St. Louis Dispatch*, dramatizes how Gandhi focused the eyes of the world on a seemingly small issue. This one campaign had giant implications. Who controls a natural substance like salt? Gandhi did not want to control it, as one looking at the cartoon might surmise. Instead, he decided to challenge the British right to a saline monopoly and the laws that imposed control on this basic product of the sea.

The context is worth noting. The All-India Congress had accepted a resolution calling for independence and secession from British rule. Gandhi realized that the burden to lead India in that direction fell upon him. As he pondered his options, he knew he would have to include civil disobedience. However, he wanted it to be framed in a nonviolent way—a true satyagraha movement. It took almost two months for him to come to a decision. The focus was to be on the Salt Act. He wrote a letter to the viceroy, Lord Irwin, the British administrator of India, informing him that the planned action would begin in nine days. Here is part of the rationale that Gandhi presented to the viceroy, with the salutation: *"Dear Friend…*

> …let me put before you some of the salient points. The terrific pressure of land revenue, which furnishes a large part of the total, must undergo considerable modification in an independent India…The whole revenue system has to be revised as to make the peasant's good its primary concern. But the British system seems to be designed to crush the very life out of him. Even the salt he must use to live is so taxed as to make the burden fall heaviest on him, if only because of the heartless impartiality of its incidence. The tax shows itself still more burdensome on the poor man when it is remembered that the salt is the one thing he must eat more than the rich man. The drink and

drug revenue, too, is derived from the poor. It saps the foundations both of their health and morals.

Gandhi realized he could be arrested ahead of the march, but although Lord Irwin replied with a curt letter of disapproval, he made no move to incarcerate him. True to Gandhi's word, the Salt March started from the Sabarmati ashram in western India with seventy-eight marchers. The group walked south through rural villages, two hundred and forty miles, to the seacoast village of Dandi, on the Gulf of Cambay. Because Gandhi had made known that he would undertake this action, people across India were focused on the Salt March, and lined the roads to see him. Several thousand people joined the walkers. Many foreign journalists came to cover the march. Arun Gandhi, describes the scene in *The Forgotten Woman*:

> For the next three and a half weeks, the whole world charted the progress of Mahatma Gandhi and his pilgrims. Newsreels showed a gaunt old man in shawl and dhoti striding along on matchstick legs at a pace that tested the stamina of his most youthful followers. News photos pictured him addressing huge crowds of onlookers who knelt beside the road, or perched on walls and rooftops, even in treetops, in each village the marchers passed through.

A large crowd was at the scene as Gandhi waded into the water and returned to shore. During low tide, puddles of water remain along the coast. The scorching sun dries them up, causing salt deposits to appear. Gandhi picked up a handful of this sea salt in open violation of British law. This provided the initial signal for massive civil disobedience by other Indians. Soon it seemed the whole country was processing salt. There was brutal retaliation by the army against unarmed nonviolent protesters at a salt works factory, and it stirred the conscience of the world. With the international media on the scene reporting and exposing these events, the British Empire was shaken to its moral foundation. Thousands of his followers, along with Gandhi himself, went to jail.

Through Gandhi's simple yet dramatic action, people around the world came to understand that the mighty British government had been forced to its knees by public opinion. While independence for India was still seventeen years away, the stage for self-rule was being set by a diminutive man with almost no physical resources, but with a strong belief in nonviolent action.

While living in South Africa, Gandhi had made it clear that his intentions were not to win freedom for India at any cost. His goal was nobler, and the means to the goal was to have a peaceful transition. He wrote:

> India's greatest glory will consist not in regarding Englishmen as her implacable enemies fit only to be turned out of India at the first available opportunity but in turning them into friends and partners in a new commonwealth of nations in the place of an empire based upon exploitation of the weaker or underdeveloped nations and races of the earth.

★★★

As was true with the British government's reaction to Gandhi's initiative in rejecting the salt tax, when a government seeks to retaliate or force its will on another nation or on its own people, it may appear to succeed in the short run, but history has a way of correcting the abuse. For example, this was true of the U.S. intervention in Nicaragua, which fostered a civil war. The eventual revelation of secret Iran-Contra funding was a great embarrassment to the United States and many elected officials were ashamed that a secret war had been waged with consent from the White House.

The story of the Greek-owned vessel dumping its sickening cargo in residential areas is a dramatic example of commerce without morality. In the age of the World Bank and the IMF, the perspectives of liberation theology grow increasingly important in Sri Lanka, Nicaragua, the Ivory Coast, and every other developing country.

The intricate connection of politics and religion reflect how Gandhi approached his work; he saw himself as a religious reformer and made decisions based upon spiritual values. The ethical issues of globalization include stewardship of all the physical resources of the land, sea, and air. Given the principle of swadeshi, it is safe to conclude that Gandhi would draw on the principle of self-sufficiency if he were asked to give advice about commerce to the United States today. He might encourage support for local communities and the farmers and small businesses found there.

One of my daughters has a bumper sticker on her car that reads BE A LOCAL HERO—BUY LOCALLY GROWN. Today, many Community Supported Agriculture groups and food cooperatives are thriving. Growing numbers of people limit their consumption primarily to food produced in their own region. Gandhi would endorse these movements and encourage them to expand. Local credit unions might also receive his approval—many of these financial institutions support the local community with low-interest loans offered exclusively to residents in surrounding neighborhoods. Credit unions, by not engaging in the sub-prime mortgage lending that took loans far beyond local communities, had little role in the 2007 financial collapse, a crisis whose tentacles are deeply affecting countries throughout the world.

> "India need not be drawn into the vortex of mad and ruinous competition which breeds fratricide, jealousy, and many other evils." —Gandhi

Lord Willingdon's Dilemma

Lord Freeman Thomas Willingdon, the viceroy of India, is caught in the toils of satyagraha. On July 15, 1933, Gandhi sent him a wire asking for an interview to explore the possibility of a peaceful and honorable settlement of the differences between the congress and the government on the question of constitutional reforms. Willingdon refused the request, and Sir Samuel Hoare, British Secretary of State for India, told the House of Commons:

> We have said that we are not prepared to negotiate, and we shall maintain that position. Mr. Gandhi wishes to put himself in the position of negotiations with the government of India and also carries in reserve the unconditional weapon of civil disobedience. I repeat that there can be no question of making a bargain with the congress as a condition for their accepting the ordinary obligations of law abiding citizens. (1932)

Four

Science Without Humanity

If we make new discoveries and inventions in the phenomenal world, must we declare our bankruptcy in the spiritual domain? Is it impossible to multiply the exceptions so as to make them the rule? Must man always be brute first and man after, if at all? —Gandhi

Gandhi was forty years old in 1909 when, having become the leader of the satyagraha movement on behalf of Indians in South Africa, he returned to London on his second mission for this cause. It was during this visit that he began to reflect upon the cultures of Eastern and Western civilizations, and he wrote an article about these ideas called *Confession of Faith*. It included fifteen statements that he later expanded to greater length in *Hind Swaraj*. A few of his observations from *Confessions of Faith* are worth considering:

—The people of Europe, before they were touched with modern civilization, had much in common with the people of the East.
—Increase of material comforts is not in any way whatsoever conducive to moral growth.

—India's salvation consists in unlearning what she has learned during the past fifty years, in that the upper classes have to learn-conscientiously, religiously, and deliberately-the simple peasant life, knowing it to be a life-giving true happiness.

Never claiming to be a model of consistency, Gandhi always reserved the right to change his mind, and he frequently did. For example, on the question of a nation's right to use force, he was initially ambivalent. Gandhi was often skeptical about scientific advances, including a negative view of doctors and Western medicine, especially in his younger years. In time, he dismissed some of his concerns on this subject after medical doctors helped him recover from appendicitis and weakness brought on by fasting. He spent a good deal of energy nursing sick people with natural cures, such as mudpacks, specific diets, and water baths. Gandhi was also skeptical of many modern inventions. He was very cautious about new kinds of machinery, such as the automobile, that purported to make life easier. Part of this may have been his concern about the moral implications of replacing spiritual values with material possessions.

Pacifist Evolution

Gandhi saw a patriotic role for himself and his fellow Indians in South Africa by supporting the British army. Gandhi believed that the British rule of law, while not without its faults, was the best in the world. While this may seem at odds with reason, Gandhi perceived that India could be a Commonwealth country with ties to Britain, but not under its direct rule. Thus, during the Second Boer War (1899-1902), while his sympathies were with the less powerful Dutch farmers (Boers), he still felt obliged to participate in support of the British Empire. In both the Boer War and the Zulu Rebellion, Gandhi's ambulance crew assisted the British by carrying stretchers over many miles. He led the team of volunteers on dangerous missions to bring wounded men from both sides off of the battlefields and back to a base hospital. While it never involved actual fighting, the work was often very dangerous, and the sacrifice involved was duly noted. For these efforts, Gandhi was awarded medals of bravery by Britain.

As World War I broke out, Gandhi tried to enlist his countrymen in England to serve as medics for Britain. In that effort, he met great resistance from fellow Indians, who saw contradictions between his widely known satyagraha teachings and military recruitment. He was challenged on his nonviolent principles. Perhaps the struggle was also within him, because he became ill at this time. Gandhi soon recognized that his willingness to compromise in support of the British cause had taken a heavy toll on his physical health, and he understood more fully why it was a point of concern for others. He withdrew his recruiting effort, moved back to India, and spent a long period in physical recovery.

Gandhi felt a lingering attachment to the British Empire that caused his ambivalence. His awareness of the power of peaceful resistance had become evident earlier in his public involvement in South Africa. Like other aspects of his personal beliefs, his thinking on nonviolence and pacifism evolved over time, and long before the foreboding shadow of World War II, Gandhi's antiwar position reached certainty within himself. By the start of World War II he was appalled at the growing global arsenal of powerful weapons. The regional threat of Japanese invasion hung over India. Gandhi's refusal to support mobilization of an Indian army caused a split with many of his supporters and political allies in the Indian National Congress, yet he always tried to understand and respect their position, as he did of Indians who chose to fight with the British.

Gandhi was stunned when he heard that atomic bombs had been dropped on Hiroshima and Nagasaki. Some American friends suggested to him that the atomic bomb would bring non-violence in its wake. He responded to that argument by asking: "What difference does it make to the dead, the orphans and the homeless, whether the mad destruction is wrought under the name of totalitarianism or the holy name of liberty or democracy?"

Gandhi came to understand that greed was one of the underlying roots of war. He valued simplicity and the sharing of possessions, and he came to model this thinking in his actions. For example, moving from the lifestyle of a successful lawyer to voluntarily adopting a simple, pedant style of dress took place over time. He eventually saw the decision to wear plain clothing as part of a political movement in India, and he urged politicians to follow suit.

In Gandhi's transition from limited participation in military actions to complete pacifism, he went through various phases. Even in the early stages, while he appreciated the discipline of military training, teaching aggression to recruits caused him some concern. When a voice of conscience in military life was stifled it bothered Gandhi, but it was the violence of war that eventually brought him to an absolute refusal to take part, even in a humane, supportive role.

★★★

My perspective on violence and war has also evolved. I was twelve years old when I heard that an atom bomb was dropped over Japan. It seemed like a good thing from my perspective at the time, within a culture of acceptance in family, neighborhood, and school; it prompted the hope that the war would soon be completely over.

As the debate on the morality of using nuclear weapons has unfolded through the years, my opinion has changed. Considering Augustine's just-war theory and alternative pacifist positions from Christian perspectives, I began to understand the devastation and horror of bombing civilian populations, no matter what the intended goal. As with Gandhi, I came to believe that the end does not justify the means. Using a nuclear weapon that indiscriminately destroys populations of people is evil. The just-war condition of discrimination, which states that noncombatants cannot be directly attacked, is impossible in a nuclear attack.

My opposition to the conventional war-making mentality came slowly. The requirement of defending one's country seemed reasonable, so giving government leaders the benefit of the doubt, when they declared our participation in wars, seemed a patriotic thing to do. I signed on as a chaplain for the New York Air National Guard—nicknamed locally, "The Boys from Syracuse"—during the Vietnam War, and came close to being called into active duty. As it turned out, only half the unit was mobilized at that time, and the chaplain's role was not included.

As I have grown in acceptance and appreciation of nonviolence, I have come to the point of questioning all wars. Like the German moral theologian, Bernard Haring, I realize that there always will be a need for peacekeepers throughout the world, but there also is a healing power in an active, pacifist approach to violence. I believe that other than a peacekeeping role, war is unnecessary and immoral.

United States Marine Major General Smedley D. Butler was a two-time winner of the Congressional Medal of Honor. Butler said that his war experiences in China, Nicaragua, Cuba, and Haiti, where intervention was primarily motivated by protection for American corporations, allowed him to understand how profit is the underlying reason for war. He came to believe that: "War is a racket. It always has been. It is possibly the oldest, easily the most profitable, surely the most vicious. It is the only one international in scope. It is the only one in which the profits are reckoned in dollars and the losses in lives."

Butler's slender book *War Is a Racket* was first published in 1935. While the initial focus is on financial benefits to a few corporations and individuals, the eventual reality about who ends up paying the bills rests squarely on the soldiers. From Butler's experience:

> Boys with a normal viewpoint were taken out of the fields, offices, factories, and classrooms, and put into the ranks. There, they were remolded; they were made over; they were made to "about face" and to regard murder as the order of the day. They were put shoulder to shoulder, and through mass psychology, they were entirely changed. We used them for a couple of years and trained them to think nothing at all of killing or of being killed. Then, suddenly, we discharged them and told them to make another 'about face!'

Means and Ends

While he knew that politics could play a positive role, his life experiences had taught him caution as a political leader. Gandhi had a firm belief that the means of pursuing a goal is equally as important as the goal itself, "They say 'means are after all (just) means,' I would say 'means are after all everything.' As the means, so the end…there is no wall of separation between means and end." Gandhi maintained a degree of skepticism that set him apart from many politicians, as means and ends were convertible terms for him.

In the Hebrew scriptures, the story of Joseph the Dreamer, described in the Book of Genesis, provides insight into the phenomenon of turning away from unpleasant actions, even our own. The brothers of Joseph were so angry with their younger brother, who was favored by their father, that they wanted to kill him. Instead, because of the intervention of one sibling, Reuben, they agreed to throw him into a dry cistern, which was not exactly a nonviolent response. "Then," the author tells us, "they sat down to eat." (Gen. 37: 25) This story seems an appropriate metaphor for how some of us may feel after media exposure of domestic or foreign violence. Do we not feel frustrated, but continue what we are doing without any further action? Is that not also what we do in paying our federal taxes without protest, at the same time realizing that some of our tax dollars are being used for destructive purposes and even to cover up atrocities? We sit down to eat, but our meal is not always digestible.

Gandhi wrestled with the same questions and responded in nonviolent ways. During much of his life, the end goal of freedom-minded Indians was independence from Britain. They wanted that objective badly, but as a leader, Gandhi never chose immoral or dubious means, political or otherwise, to achieve it. That set him apart from many other leaders. Yet, it gave to the world a witness that the means should always be in harmony with the desired end.

Pax Christi

I have come to believe that making a decision to stand against war requires a strong appreciation for the effectiveness of nonviolence. *Pax Christi* (Latin for peace of Christ) is an international organization that encourages members to commit to a nonviolent lifestyle. It was founded after World War II by groups of women from France and Germany who recognized the need for reconciliation between the two nations and began meeting toward that end. My wife and I came to know the group in England in the mid-1970s. Around that time, in part through the efforts of the Benedictine Sisters in Erie, Pennsylvania, an American branch of Pax Christi was established. A local chapter was founded in Syracuse in 1978.

On the 50th anniversary of the bombings of Hiroshima and Nagasaki, in August 1995, members of Pax Christi Syracuse undertook a two-week pilgrimage across upstate New York. Starting at a nuclear storage facility in Romulus, we walked through rural areas, villages, and cities. The group developed more discipline when it was joined by Jun San, a Buddhist nun who has vast experience in walking long distances to raise awareness of peace and justice issues. The march ended with one hundred and forty participants at a peace pagoda outside of Troy. A Hiroshima survivor, twelve years old at the time of the bombing, spoke at the closing ceremony. He encouraged our group to work to eliminate nuclear weapons.

One of the vital aspects of Pax Christi is to encourage members to take a yearly pledge of nonviolence. Recognizing the violence in my own heart, I considered it thoroughly before making the personal decision to take this vow:

> Before God the Creator and the Sanctifying Spirit, I vow to carry out in my life the love and example of Jesus:
> by striving for peace within myself and seeking to be a peacemaker in my daily life;
> by accepting suffering rather than inflicting it;

by refusing to retaliate in the face of provocation and violence;

by persevering in nonviolence of tongue and heart;

by living conscientiously and simply so that I do not deprive others of the means to live; and

by actively resisting evil and working nonviolently to abolish war and the causes of war from my own heart and from the face of the earth.

Nuclear Shadow

The biblical idea of beating swords into plowshares was the driving force behind a meeting of Vietnam War resisters in the late 1960s. A group of peace activists, including Philip and Daniel Berrigan, gathered at a retreat center in upstate New York to begin a discussion on civil disobedience. The likely consequence of a direct action was a felony conviction. Those who were not American citizens faced deportation. As a participant in that retreat, I was impressed by the strong commitment to nonviolence and the willingness to take risks to promote peace.

For over forty years Philip Berrigan, who died from cancer in 2002, was a forceful leader in the civil rights and anti-war movement. In part stemming from his experiences as a soldier in World War II, Phil opposed violence and found the military to be a racist institution. He saw the violence of war and military spending as directly contradicting his belief in God. Along with his brothers Dan and Jerome, he was willing to accept jail time as a consequence of direct actions to raise awareness of nuclear danger, the sinful dimension of building a nuclear arsenal, the great tragedy of war, and how a budget dominated by military spending negatively impacts the poor. In 1980, Phil and Dan launched the Plowshares Movement when they entered a General Electric nuclear missile plant in Pennsylvania, hammered on nuclear warheads, poured blood on documents, and prayed. Since then, there have been nearly eighty Plowshare actions. Phil participated in several and spent, cumulatively, over eleven years in prison.

Phil personified the gospel message everyday in his life at Jonah House, a Catholic Worker community in Baltimore, where he lived with his wife and fellow activist Elizabeth McAllister, their children, and community members committed to lives of service and non-materialism. In many ways, Phil followed in Gandhi's path, letting go of self in order to serve the greater good. In an interview, he explained his thoughts on power and powerlessness:

We should recall as frequently as possible that the temptations of Christ in the desert (as recorded by Matthew and Luke), which are stereotypes of all human temptations, are really temptations to power, whether religious, economic or political power. We need to remember that our Lord did not succumb to those temptations to power. The alternative to succumbing to the temptation of power is to embrace powerlessness. One then becomes an agency through which the power of God can work. One becomes a vehicle for divine power. But that means that the ego has to be suppressed along with its natural instinct to power. We have to deny the self, take up the cross and follow. We have to embrace powerlessness.

Phil's funeral was held at St. Peter Claver church in Baltimore, a parish where he had ministered and had once hung a banner reading: "The sting of death is all around us. O Christ, where is your victory?" In this message, McAllister said, he was referring not to a personal death but to death facilitated by nations at war. Phil used his life force in a way that always considered the greater good. In a way, his whole being embodied satyagraha. The program for his funeral liturgy included a quote from Dorothy Day, written shortly after the bombing of Hiroshima and Nagasaki:

> Down in Washington, a conference is beginning. The great ones of the earth are conferring. The very scientists that brought forth the atomic bomb are the most afraid of all of what is to come. What to do? We can only suggest one thing—destroy the two billion dollars worth of equipment that was built to make the atomic bomb, destroy all the formulas, put on sack cloth and ashes, and weep and repent.

As the debate continues about obtaining, building, using, and stockpiling nuclear weapons, the world is caught in the dilemma that Day described. The division between politics and religion is blurred to participants in Plowshares actions and others driven by faith to challenge militarism. Another beacon of awareness about nuclear danger was Richard McSorley S.J., Jesuit theologian at Georgetown University, World War I veteran, pioneering Catholic Worker, and close friend of the Kennedys. McSorley used his academic and theological perspectives to forge a new path in Peace Studies. One of McSorley's most famous books suggests that it is a sin to build a nuclear weapon; just as with Gandhi and the Ploughshares activists, staying true to his principles was a way of being for him. Regardless of religious beliefs, one consequence of the United States' commitment to building up nuclear weapons and stockpiles has been its loss of moral authority to dictate to other countries what they can and cannot do to obtain such nuclear materials and technologies.

★★★

In August 2005, The *Syracuse Post-Standard* published my op-ed piece under the headline: "Nuclear Club Members Lack Moral Authority."

> The 60th anniversary of the development and first use of atomic and nuclear weapons this month has presented us with a time for serious reflection. Several of the scientists who worked on the Manhattan Project later expressed regret for participating in the development of these immoral weapons.
>
> Once the genie was out of the bottle, our leaders in Washington began scrambling on how to maintain, restrict, or modify this destructive power. We are still scrambling.
>
> As other nations learned the nuclear formula, they sought to keep up with the USA—always for "national defense." Now, more and more countries want to try joining the nuclear club, much to the dismay of the so-called nuclear powers. We admonish them—India, Pakistan, North Korea, Iran—but with what moral authority?
>
> Likewise, we abhor the use of other methods of warfare, like the suicide bombings that indiscriminately kill civilians as well as military personnel. Yet, our country

lacks the moral force to speak against them with a convincing voice.

If the United States would stop further development of nuclear weapons and begin to model their elimination, there would be new hope for a world that has existed and continues to exist under a nuclear shadow. The present mayor of Hiroshima has pleaded for all nuclear powers to abandon their deadly arsenals, saying that the United States, Russia, and other members of the nuclear club are 'jeopardizing human survival.'

Violence Begets Violence

In 1988, the explosion of an American commercial aircraft over Scotland took the lives of hundreds of innocent individuals; among them were thirty-five Syracuse University students returning home after a semester abroad. The impact on the Syracuse community was huge-terrorism had hit home. Ten years after the tragedy, I sent this letter to the editor of *The Post Standard*:

> The 10th anniversary memorial service at Syracuse University put a human face on the Pan Am 103 tragedy at Lockerbie, Scotland. The tolling of the bell while naming each Central New York victim was a poignant reminder of the pain that families and friends have experienced since that event.
>
> In the ensuing cry to bring the responsible terrorists to justice, it is all but forgotten that what preceded that terrible act by less than six months was a tragedy of at least equal proportion. On July 3, 1988, while patrolling the Persian Gulf, the United States cruise ship, *Vincennes*, blew out of the sky a commercial airliner coming out of Iran. It was officially labeled "a mistake," with Captain Rogers explaining that he couldn't identify it immediately. The family and friends of the 290 individuals must have felt the same pain and anguish over the past decade as was manifested last week in Hendricks Chapel.
>
> Was the bombing of the Pan Am 103 an act of retaliation? We may or may not find that out someday. We do know that violence begets violence, as we experience time and time again in our nation and in our neighborhoods.
>
> The human face of the violence we have inflicted upon Iraq over the past eight years, through economic sanctions and cruise missiles, may not be evident to most of us in America. But it is very evident to the Iraqi people and to their Arab neighbors. We know not how it will come back

upon us, but we can only sadly speculate that, sooner or later, it will.

In this Christmas season and time of Ramadan, as we pray for peace on Earth, we need to back up our prayers with actions that will lead to healing and reconciliation. We have a long road to travel.

The headline "Violence Provides No Closure: Pan-Am 103 Tragedy May Be Part of Vicious Circle" has proven sadly true as the American invasions of Iraq and Afghanistan and the subsequent wars have unfolded. Even before the current Iraq war, spent uranium from bombs used during the first Gulf War had poisoned Iraqi citizens, including many children:

> Iraqi and visiting doctors, and a number of news reports, have reported that birth defects and cancers in Iraqi children have increased five- to 10-fold since the 1991 Gulf War and continue to increase sharply, to over 30-fold in some areas in southern Iraq. Currently, more than 50 percent of Iraqi cancer patients are children under the age of 5, up from 13 percent. Children are especially vulnerable because they tend to play in areas that are heavily polluted by depleted uranium.

How can the costs of the Iraqi or Afghan war be measured? From vantage points all over the globe, people have access to information from a wide range of media outlets and are examining both the short-term and long-term consequences. In drawing a conclusion, it should be remembered that an ever-increasing number are measuring the staggering costs of these wars in a very personal way.

★★★

Sordid tales of abuse in American run prisons in Iraq reflect a moral decay connected to the concept of science without humanity. The exposure of inmate abuse at Abu Ghraib prison brought into living rooms around the world the realization that the military personnel involved in these incidents seemed to have lost all sense of right and wrong. Some of the guards went so far as to document their abuse in incriminating photographs, not only to shame and intimidate the prisoners but also to brag about inflicting torture.

A secondary outcome of torture involves the effect it has on the individual who administers it. Research reveals the detrimental mental health consequences on torturers themselves. Veterans' hospitals and divorce courts provide anecdotal evidence of this as well. Even beyond those directly involved, consider what torture does to the collective psyche. Yet, when a military or government attempts to shield ordinary citizens from the brutal treatment of prisoners, victims in places like Abu Ghraib, Guantanamo, and Bagram in Afghanistan belie their efforts. The question we need to ask is; what does this do to a nation's soul?

Trying to justify various methods of torture in the name of national security exposes a government to harsh criticism from those who see patterns of abuse from a different perspective. Archbishop Desmond Tutu, in a British radio interview, stated that he never imagined that he would live to see the day when the United States and its satellites would use precisely the same arguments that South African proponents of apartheid used for detention without trial.

The psychology that allows individuals to justify abuse has been studied from the perspectives of various disciplines. Howard Thurman shared his insights from a ministerial point of view in his book, *Jesus and the Disinherited*. Written more than a quarter of a century ago, it explains how ordinary military security personnel can allow themselves to become morally twisted. It begins with developing a hatred of the enemy so strong that it immunizes individuals from a loss of self-respect. Thurman uses the analogy of a curtain being dropped "in front of their moral values and ethical integrity as human beings and as Americans, and they moved around in front of the curtain to do their death-dealing work on other human beings."

Psychiatrist Rollo May, in his book *Power and Innocence: A Search for the Sources of Violence*, makes a similar point, saying "At the outset of every war, we hastily transform the enemy into the image of the demoniac, and then, since it is the devil we are fighting, we can shift into a war without asking ourselves all the troublesome psychological and spiritual questions that war arouses." In so many areas, both in personal conduct and in the building and stockpiling of weapons of mass destruction, scientific knowledge has outpaced spiritual awareness.

As countries have scrambled to obtain or contain weapons of mass destruction, individual voices have been muted in their condemnation. Gandhi observed, "So far as I can see, the atomic bomb has deadened the finest feeling that has sustained mankind for ages. There used to be the so-called laws of war that made it tolerable. Now, we know the naked truth. War knows no law except that of might."

The willingness of the United States to develop a nuclear weapon in the Manhattan Project was seen by many as a brave step forward for science. The desire to bring an end to World War II was noble, but in hindsight, developing a weapon of mass destruction was an immoral, and many historians believe an unnecessary, means to bring the war to a conclusion. From the use of the first atomic bomb on Hiroshima, the struggle to contain the information and tools necessary to construct these weapons has proven to be a nightmare that goes on and on. When India acquired the capacity to build a nuclear weapon, long after Gandhi's death, Pakistan felt the need to do likewise; today an ominous nuclear threat hangs over both countries.

Declaring a preemptive war on Iraq without evidence of a true threat to the United States has shown itself to be disastrous and ethically wrong. Deterring Saddam Hussein from developing weapons of mass destruction was clearly desirable by nations everywhere. But it appears in retrospect that no such nuclear program existed. Once again, the use of immoral means toward a shared goal proved destructively self-defeating.

A recent addition to the United States' military arsenal is unmanned aerial assault weaponry, commonly known as drones. These are deployed on reconnaissance and bombing missions. Voices for Creative Nonviolence, a nonprofit based in Chicago, describes the remote control system in which pilots and bombardiers direct operations from positions on the other side of the globe:

Now, using 'eyes in the skies' by piloting unmanned aerial vehicles (drones), the United States can see and attack suspected Taliban fighters, along with anyone else who might be in the vicinity, in Afghanistan and Pakistan. But all of our 'eyes in the skies,' performing constant surveillance, will never help us see our opponents as potential neighbors. We'll never really see them at all, as humans who must never be mistaken for objects, until we cast away our weapons.

Voices for Creative Nonviolence sent delegations to Iraq as civilian observers during the build-up and the shock-and-awe periods of the U.S. invasion of Iraq. Others were more recently in Pakistan, experiencing firsthand the fear that is engendered by families when the sound of drones circling the sky above reaches their ears.

The drones, which are nicknamed Predator and Reaper, raise ethical questions concerning science without humanity, technology without consideration of unintended consequences, and war without measuring collateral damage. Shortly after Barack Obama was inaugurated he carried out several decisive actions to move the country in a new direction. However, Obama's decision to allow the use and further development of the drone operation is out of step with other, more peaceful decisions that he has made, as well as his anti-war campaign image.

Long time Pentagon strategist Pierre Sprey, appearing on *Bill Moyers Journal* in January 2009, noted that in his judgment, the capability of drones is "enormously exaggerated." The aircraft is relatively slow and bulky. One of its purposes is surveillance, and the plane's cameras can zero in on faces below, but it also carries 500-pound bombs. Using its weaponry to target an enemy combatant from a distance, Spray said, usually has severe unintended consequences: "I'd be astonished if one of five people they kill or wound is in fact a militant."

Behind Bars

How did Gandhi carry out the principle of noncooperation in his own life? When he was faced with dilemmas that could not be resolved through discourse, such as deadlocked deliberations on proposed laws that would discriminate against Indians in South Africa, he protested by refusing to cooperate with the statute and going to prison. His example inspired many other Indians to do the same, with the result that the prisons became full to overflowing, and the issues involved were often reconsidered. The same dynamic later took place in India.

The history of Gandhi's jail time is worth noting. In South Africa, where he first experienced prison at age thirty-eight, sentences were shorter - his initial sentence was two months. Later that year he was arrested again and given another two-month sentence. This time, seventy-five compatriots joined him. In prison Gandhi read *Civil Disobedience* by Henry David Thoreau and was deeply impressed. When Thoreau declared, "I did not feel for a moment confined, and the walls seemed a great waste of stone and mortar," Gandhi wholeheartedly agreed. He served two additional three-month sentences in South Africa in the campaign against the Black Law. With both women and men willing to face imprisonment, the movement succeeded. Legislation was modified, and compromises were reached.

In India, Gandhi's jail sentences were much longer; his writing in *Young India* brought a charge of sedition. For this he received a six-year sentence, although he ended up serving just two years, as he was released for medical reasons after an operation for acute appendicitis. In 1930, in the aftermath of the dramatic march to the sea, Gandhi was again arrested and imprisoned under an ordinance. There was no trial, no sentence, no fixed term. He was released ten months later. A year later, Gandhi, now sixty-two, was placed in Yeravda jail, where he remained for thirteen months.

In 1932, Gandhi had just returned to India from England, where he had represented the Indian Congress at a high-level conference and been entertained in Buckingham palace. Upon his return he was jailed; his "crime" was a negative response to a new set of restrictive laws the British were enacting. The cartoon of Lord Willingdon's Dilemma, (page 55) which appeared in the *Hindustan Times*, gives some idea of how decisions by the British government to imprison Gandhi had huge political implications. (Lord Willingdon was the viceroy, the top representative of the British Empire in India.) What prompted Gandhi's arrest was his suggestion that perhaps civil disobedience might be needed, the mere idea of which caused the viceroy to panic. Gandhi requested a visit with Lord Willingdon, but was refused. After Gandhi's arrest, other leaders in the Indian Congress were jailed along with over 32,000 others. As a result the jails were overflowing. This became Lord Willingdon's dilemma and, in effect, because of Gandhi's fame, the dilemma of the British Empire.

The cartoon displays a powerful irony. Far from eliminating the threat of disruption among the populace, as Lord Willingdon assumed, the arrest of one man with strong moral principles inspired others to accept the same consequences. This caused the British government great embarrassment. Since Gandhi's time, the same scenario has been repeated to one degree or another throughout the world, whenever people participate in noncooperation and accept imprisonment for political reasons.

While most of those arrested found prison an interruption to daily living and thus difficult, for Gandhi it often felt like a period of respite. At Yeravda he rejected offers of special treatment by the prison administrators and used his time to put finishing touches on his short book about God and the efficacy of prayer. Gandhi's final imprisonment was in Yeravda from August 1942 until February 1944. Kasturba was also imprisoned there at that time, for supporting her husband, and it was where she died with Gandhi at her side. All told, Gandhi spent six and a half years in prison over a thirty-six year period.

Gandhi's message to America today on the social sin of science without humanity might include the same thoughts he shared in his publications and speeches in the first half of the 20th century. Perhaps he would tell us that while scientific advancements have often been a boon to humanity, the common good should always be considered. He would most likely encourage

America to reduce its military forces, radically reduce the military budget, and eliminate nuclear weapons. He might suggest that if we were to stop stockpiling these destructive weapons, we might be an example to the rest of the world. If he were to visit, he would likely encourage youth to improve their scientific knowledge, applying it to the pressing issues of ecology and climate change for our health as well as the health of the more than 1.7 million species on our globe.

> The moral to be legitimately drawn from the supreme tragedy of the bomb is that it will not be destroyed by counter-bombs, even as violence cannot be by counter-violence. Humankind has to get out of violence only through nonviolence. Hatred can be overcome only by love. Counter-hatred only increases the surface as well as the depth of hatred. —Gandhi

The European and American press reported the civil disobedience movement extensively and with deep sympathy. Cartoonists in these countries also took up the cause of Indian independence. In this drawing, which appeared in *Kladderadatsch*, a very popular humorous weekly of Berlin between the two world wars, India is shown moving inexorably toward freedom under the guidance of Gandhi, despite the frantic efforts of the British establishment to halt it by brute force. (1922)

Five

Knowledge Without Character

> "There are moments in your life when you must act even though you cannot carry your best friends with you. The still small voice within you must always be the final arbiter when there is a conflict of duty." - Gandhi

Gandhi had a dream for India. It included many of the movements that he pursued and wrote about in his weekly newspapers and journals. His constructive program for India included three central themes: Hindu-Muslim unity, untouchability, and swadeshi. Nevertheless, he also worked on many other causes. When he was sixty-one, he wrote:

> I shall work for an India...in which there shall be no high class and low class of people, an India in which all communities shall live in perfect harmony. There can be no room in such an India for the curse of untouchability or the curse of intoxicating drinks and drugs. Women shall enjoy the same rights as men. Since we shall be at peace with all the rest of the world neither exploiting nor being exploited, we should have the smallest army imaginable.

Andrews, like others trained in Gandhi's ashram, traveled to villages across India to share Gandhi's program on *ahimsa* (non-harm). In his biography of Gandhi, Andrews describes a way to explain Gandhi's reform program by holding up his hand and pointing out the five fingers along with the wrist. The wrist symbolized nonviolence as the central uniting factor. Each finger was identified with one of Gandhi's basic platforms. First was the removal of untouchability; second, the prohibition of alcohol and drugs; third, the equality of women and men; fourth, Hindu-Muslim unity; and fifth, the encouragement of home spinning.

★★★

In his autobiography, Gandhi shared embarrassing information about himself. Gandhi was brutally honest in revealing material that no one else could have known, including some painful incidents that involved harsh treatment of his wife when they were young. Neither did he hesitate to share his youthful indiscretions. His ego was never at stake; he was focused on honesty in his ongoing experiments with truth. Even in his late sixties, he wrote in *Harijan* about a sexual temptation that came to him in a dream, which prompted him to apply additional discipline on himself. In his desire to assist others in their earthly struggles, Gandhi revealed this kind of information about himself. His life was an open book, and he wanted to avoid any cunning or deceit as he responded to others' needs.

Gandhi revered justice. Although he revealed many of his human failings, he sought to be a just man as a husband, a father, a lawyer, a member of various extended families and a civic and political leader. As a practicing lawyer, he facilitated mediation and mutual agreement rather than punishment. In an effort to be completely objective, he gave few educational privileges to his sons and did not always make life easy for his wife. These flaws were balanced by his own efforts at self-discipline and his continual attempts to be a fair and peaceful person. He came to believe that the way to peace came about only through a nonviolent route. Gandhi understood that the means to that peace came at a sacrifice, one that he was willing to make again and again by fasting and accepting periods of jail time.

Gandhi was also a man of considerable knowledge. Throughout his life he was a prolific writer. He did not see himself as particularly gifted intellectually, but as his critic and friend, G.K. Gokhale, said of him, "Gandhi has in him the marvelous spiritual power to turn ordinary men around him into heroes and martyrs," and added that in his presence, "One is ashamed to do anything unworthy, afraid of thinking anything unworthy."

Gandhi labored to teach his sons truth and honesty, sometimes expecting too much of them in their youthful development. Kasturba corrected him when she thought he was overly demanding of his young children, and he learned to accept her criticisms and to address them. This helped him to be more lighthearted with the other children in the ashram communities. They responded in turn and were greatly attracted to him.

In his pursuit of the development of character, Gandhi held out ideals that were not always easy for his followers to embrace. He seemed to believe that it is the character of a person that determines how knowledge, once gained, is put to use in life, and that a person's character is far more important than intellectual gifts. That is one reason that he was attracted to this particular social sin - knowledge without character.

Assessing the Law

Gandhi's early attempts in the legal arena were failures. It was only after accepting a case in South Africa and getting involved in civil rights activities that his skills began to emerge. Gandhi used his knowledge of law in satyagraha actions and to analyze how the legal system discriminated against those with little power or wealth.

In Gandhi's first year back in India, he followed his mentor Gokhale's advice and spent a year reacquainting himself with his homeland before looking for an opportunity to address issues of inequality and colonialism. He began his first satyagraha campaign in India after a persistent member of a distant, isolated rural district, named Champaran, invited him to visit and witness how English property owners were taxing tenant farmers at an exorbitant rate. Gandhi saw the poor indigo farmers living in terrible conditions, and agreed to help. Assessing the farmers' dilemma, he observed how the law was working against them. Gandhi did not advise them to seek their rights in the courts, where he predicted that they would be crushed and fear stricken. Rather, he perceived that the farmers could best meet their objectives and regain their dignity through taking a collective stand. He shared information through newspaper articles and helped the farmers realize that they should join forces rather than risk personal intimidation. Gandhi approached the landlords to discuss the situation but they refused to meet with him, and a British commissioner ordered him to leave the region. Gandhi refused and was arrested. It was his first act of civil disobedience in India.

Gandhi and Kasturba remained in Champaran for almost a year. Kasturba taught the women of the village basic sanitary techniques and assisted Gandhi in setting up a small school for the local children. Meanwhile, the legal case against Gandhi was dropped. Gandhi was invited by the viceroy to participate in a commission to investigate the situation of the tenant farmers. The official inquiry found in favor of the tenant farmers, including a refund and abolishment of the tithe system imposed by the landowners. Civil disobedience had won the day! Gandhi was modest about this achievement, regarding it as a success, and continued to work for other Indian civil liberties.

A Monastic Reflection

Gandhi's funeral was attended by more than two million people. It is thought to have been the largest number of people ever assembled in one place for a common reason up to that time. Around the world, people were shocked to hear the news of his assassination. Gandhi, who owned only a few possessions at the time of his death, had become a global hero. Benedictine Brother David Steindl-Rast, a psychologist and anthropologist, suggests that such global heroes are needed in our time. "We need to have the values for which we stand embodied in actual persons," he says, and avers that such heroes inspire, challenge, and dare fellow citizens to put into practice praiseworthy human values necessary for our day. Furthermore, according to Steindl-Rast, these heroes have the courage to take a stand as the authority that unites and leads us by common sense, meaning our deepest consciousness, against the forces and authorities that divide rather than unite and support us.

Steindl-Rast is a monk at Mount Saviour Monastery in Elmira, New York who has spent most of his religious life outside the monastery, studying and connecting with monastic traditions of the East. While pioneering a dialogue between Christians and Buddhists, he followed the example of another well-known monk, Thomas Merton. Echoing Gandhi's unwavering respect for other religious traditions, Merton told Steindl-Rast: "We will need courage to do the opposite of everybody else."

The Indian population in South Africa, and the farmers in the smallest, most remote villages in India, came to understand that Gandhi was such a hero, one who dared to take a stand.

★★★

My connection with Mount Saviour Monastery began during the 1960s, when I was a priest in the diocese of Syracuse. I frequently visited and became a friend of the founder, Abbot Damasus Winzen, a renowned scholar in liturgy and religious art, who encouraged Steindl-Rast to pursue his interest and connections with Buddhist spirituality and monasticism. I found the abbot to be gracious with his time, and he shared with me his observations and insights from his Benedictine spiritual journey in Europe and America. His wise counsel helped me during a difficult transition period, when I made the decision to leave the active ministry.

Crisis in the Church

My judgment at the time I was leaving the priesthood, strengthened by subsequent experience, was that celibacy is a marvelous charism, but it should not be imposed, it should be a choice. It is not necessarily related to ministry. Celibacy seems to make the most sense within the context of a strong, prayerful religious community. Ecclesiastical law mandated it after the first millennium, during the flowering of the monastic tradition. I found it to be helpful in my own ministry over a ten-year period, but I eventually came to understand that it was not always spiritually relevant for many others or myself.

The recent revelations of clerical sexual abuse certainly appear to have some relationship to the current requirement of celibacy for ordination to the Catholic priesthood. In my years as a priest, I had little idea of the sexual struggles that some colleagues were experiencing, no inkling of the devastating damage that was being inflicted upon many children and adults from sexual abuse by clerics. I had no concept of the dilemma that bishops found themselves facing as many moved priests from one assignment to another, making matters worse yet somehow believing that it would solve the problem and cover up any damage to the Church's image. It is now clear that various members of the Catholic hierarchy, including bishops, cardinals and Vatican officials, should be held accountable for the devastating effects of sexual abuse in many parts of the world. It is one example of the social sin of knowledge without character, of recognizing a painful duty but refusing to face it directly. The courage shown by Gandhi in facing the truth of every situation should be an inspiration in addressing this deep issue, healing the victims when possible and pursuing the cause.

Champion for the Downtrodden

My friend Raymond McVey, a faithful priest in the Syracuse diocese, came closer to imitating the virtues of Gandhi than anyone I have personally known. In my judgment, McVey was a heroic figure such as Steindl-Rast believes is necessary for our world. McVey and I lived together for a time in inner city Syracuse. In our modest dwelling we hosted men needing refuge from the streets, a meal, and a place to lay their heads. Bunk beds began filling our living room. Our little house with one small bathroom got so crowded that we moved to a larger place on an adjacent street. That, too, became full. McVey then found an abandoned five-building tuberculosis sanatorium in a neighboring county. With a small personal loan from a local bank to purchase the property, he moved there with a handful of men. They named it Unity Acres.

Living in that rural setting, McVey proved to be a hands-on person, working daily to correct the neglected plumbing and a host of other needs. In a few short years, the number of residents -men with alcohol problems and other addictions- swelled to over a hundred. To avoid hassles and government red tape, McVey called it his own residence. At first, his new neighbors looked upon him with great suspicion, but he eventually won them over. McVey collaborated with county and state agencies and succeeded in bringing improved services to the men in their new home. He challenged the Church to attend to the needs of the poor in both urban and rural areas and raised new awareness of old problems.

When Gandhi first decided to move to a rural area and establish a farming community and ashram, he knew he was being rash and impulsive. In his heart, he believed it was the right thing to do. So, too, McVey made an impulsive decision to take a group of men from the city streets to a rural farm retreat forty miles away. Both men succeeded. This tribute to McVey in the *Catholic Sun*, published after his death in May 1995, helps explain why I consider him a hero and his life to be one of kinship with Mahatma Gandhi:

Father Raymond McVey began his priestly ministry in 1963, when the fruits of Vatican II were first being felt at the parish level. His street ministry started out at St. Lucy's parish in 1966, when the horrors of the Vietnam War were beginning to stir protests that were new to our community and to our nation. The civil rights movement was in full stride with new awareness dawning on the real effects of racism, which had pervaded our society for so long. It was not an easy time for a young Irish priest to stir up interest in new approaches to old problems.

That was one of the reasons for his success: he challenged others, but never without a willingness to challenge himself. His simple lifestyle came through in his relationships. His green sweatshirt and black work boots were authentic symbols of his hard physical work and spiritual sacrifice.

Like Gandhi, his clothing was simple, as were all the few material things in his possession. Volunteers flocked to support his work because they recognized it as authentic. Ray saw the humanity in everyone, but he felt a special Gospel call toward the poor and the downtrodden as Christ's special friends. Like Gandhi, he did not drink, but also felt a kinship with alcoholics in their struggle to regain dignity. He often expressed the opinion that if he had ever started to drink, he probably would have been an alcoholic, too. His Spartan character was reflected in his living quarters, with his tastes in food being simple and his fasting not infrequent.

As Gandhi changed the face of South Africa and India in his time, so Ray McVey had that effect on the communities where he worked. Today, it is a more friendly face, one of reconciliation, one of more awareness of the Lazarus' in our midst. His sense of humor and patience helped many troubled people to really believe that they were 'no problem'.

Social Stigmas

For Gandhi, knowledge was not an end in itself, but once he was convinced of a truth to live by, it was important for him to put it into practice. One example was his acceptance of some of Ruskin's socialist ideas, which he wasted no time in trying out in an ashram setting. Civil resistance was another area where, once he accepted the concept, he found it necessary to act when faced with unjust laws.

A great admirer of Gandhi is Jean Vanier, who has also become convinced about a truth to live by. He has followed Gandhi's path by committing himself to a special cause. Vanier, a Canadian, has worked tirelessly to bring a spiritual awareness to the needs and gifts of persons with developmental disabilities. As founder of the international community *L'Arche* (The Ark) Vanier illustrates how individuals can choose to use their knowledge to address a societal vacuum.

Vanier was born into a family of affluence; his father was the governor-general of Canada and his mother was very highly educated. Early on, Vanier aspired to be a military officer and was commissioned in the Royal Navy. Later, he decided on a teaching career, (his doctoral dissertation involved a study of Aristotle), and he seemed well on his way to professional success when he became a professor of philosophy at the University of Toronto.

Through his mother, Vanier became acquainted with a Dominican priest in France who was chaplain of a home for developmentally disabled people. In the early 1960s, the priest persuaded Vanier to help him try a different housing model for people with physical and mental deficiencies, away from the wretched conditions of government-run facilities. Vanier agreed, and with three former residents of a local institution, he set up a modest house in Trosley, a small village outside of Paris. Two of the men stayed, and their simple residential setting was established as a permanent home. Vanier, a man with a worldly background, who had immense knowledge in the fields of education and psychology, left behind prestige and found truth in living and working with the developmentally disabled. As he shared his insights into the wonder and beauty of his housemates, largely castoffs from society, others picked up their model of family living. Since 1964, L'Arche has grown to a worldwide organization with communities in forty countries. After beginning in France, the movement spread to Canada, then India, and eventually around the world.

Vanier still lives plainly and models Gandhi's example of simplicity and integrity. He now spends his time visiting L'Arche communities and giving retreats and speeches; one of his programs focuses on Gandhi's life and teaching. Vanier finds beauty in every person, especially those who seemingly have little or nothing to contribute. For Vanier, each disabled individual is a child of God, and no matter how severely damaged, each has something to give to others and to teach a family or a community. He recognizes that the disabled often have spiritual gifts that can heal those who come in contact with them. However, the experience of L'Arche has shown that many developmentally disabled people have been so personally wounded that it takes a community effort to help them realize their wholeness, sometimes over a long period of time. Their gifts are discovered by living in a community like L'Arche, where they are recognized as the core, or heart, of the family. This has been Vanier's constant theme.

★★★

For almost five years, I was the director of L'Arche Syracuse, one of sixteen L'Arche communities in the United States. Our community consists of four homes that operate with financial support from New York state and voluntary contributions. My task was to run an agency program and, at the same time, balance the family and community aspects of L'Arche. I found it to be a graced time in many ways. By sharing life with core members, the term used for those with developmental disabilities, along with the staff who chose to live with them, I experienced firsthand the truths that Vanier came to understand. Again and again, it was the core members who taught me lessons that were surprising and life giving.

To my knowledge, Vanier has never engaged in civil disobedience. Yet, he has followed Gandhi's lead in other ways. Vanier gave up his successful career as a teacher, as Gandhi had done with his thriving law practice. Vanier was open to learning from individuals who had been so rejected that they were placed in government-run institutions –his search for truth led him outside social norms, just as Gandhi's had. Another similarity is Vanier's writing and his ability to communicate. Vanier may actually have taken his central organizing cue from Gandhi, by publishing extensive newsletters and several books to share his message. This example from Vanier's newsletter is not unlike something that Gandhi might have written, "Is not one of our problems today that we have separated ourselves from the poor, the wounded, and the suffering? We have too much time to discuss and theorize and have lost the yearning for God which comes when we are faced with the suffering of people."

Vanier's vision is evident to those who live in L'Arche communities and to all those inspired to share life with its members on any level. His strong, honest character along with his light-heartedness and enjoyment of his work are reminiscent of the frequent stories about Gandhi's spirited play with the children and adults in his ashrams. Vanier has learned a truth about individuals with developmental disabilities, and he has spent his life sharing that truth with others. At the same time, he has encouraged and established communities that enrich the lives of everyone living in them. The message of Vanier is the same as the message of Gandhi; it is a basic message of love.

As Gandhi welcomed Untouchables into his ashram, Vanier welcomed the developmentally disabled into his home. In a lifetime of work, Vanier has embraced the same spirit that moved Gandhi to challenge the caste system. Gandhi and Vanier can be compared for having an instinctive understanding of human nature: a strong, insightful character, a lively sense of humor, and a serene approach to life. For many, Vanier also fits the description of heroic.

Vanier reflects upon a pyramid image that he perceives as a common viewpoint within Western cultures:

> They say it is normal that people who are competent and have power, such as teachers, intellectuals, and wealthy

owners, be 'on top,' and those who are less competent, manual laborers, immigrants, and so on, should be on the bottom…and on the very bottom of the social ladder, there are all the unemployed, people with handicaps, and especially those with mental handicaps…Pyramidal societies become places of harsh competition where each person tries to have more money, more influence, and more power. Everyone has to win whether it is in work, in school, in sports, or even in relationships. And for every person who wins and who climbs up the social ladder, many more lose and fall down into the pits of depression, discouragement, unemployment, anger, and revolt.

Indomitable Spirit

A German newspaper published the cartoon (page 77) that portrays Gandhi riding serenely on an Asian elephant. The artist sees as futile the attempt to dislodge or stop the movement of Gandhi by physical force. The fact that Gandhi was a small man, whose weight was usually around a hundred and ten pounds, highlights the reaction even further. At times, when he fasted, his weight would drop under a hundred, only to rebound slowly after the fasting ended. Even then, his spirit was lively and sense of humor intact. Throughout his life, both friends and foes recognized Gandhi as a forceful personality, but his tranquil spirit, even during the most difficult challenges, was noteworthy. Gandhi recognized that his strength was in satyagraha, in truth force, and not in any other kind of force. His sense of prayer and worship was never forced or strained, but something quite natural to him. The power of the elephant seems a fitting symbol for Gandhi's moral strength and character. The cartoon projects the serenity of Gandhi, unshaken by attacks aimed at dislodging him. His openness to forgiveness and reconciliation continued throughout his lifetime. This cartoon, published in 1922, indicates that Gandhi's message was becoming more widely known outside of India, since he was only in his early fifties at that time.

Gandhi's sense of fearlessness was something that he developed over time, and it was repeatedly and severely tested. One instance was the white mob that attacked him after disembarking from a ship in Durban, South Africa, upon his return from India. Also in South Africa, he was beaten by one of his countrymen due to differences of opinion over a voluntary registration for Indians. He was injured to a degree that it took several weeks for him to recuperate, during which time he was a guest in a Christian missionary's home, Though his assailant was known, Gandhi refused to press charges. In time, the perpetrator apologized.

Another concept related to the nonviolence that Gandhi embraced was *tapasya* (suffering). The willingness to accept suffering personally in every social justice struggle allowed him to be fearless, and Gandhi encouraged his followers to be prepared for it in every satyagraha movement. On returning to India after two decades in South Africa, Gandhi found that his country was seized with a paralyzing fear:

> I suggest to you that there is only *one* whom we have to fear; that is God. When we fear God, then we shall fear no man however high placed he may be, and if you want to follow the vow of *truth*, then fearlessness is absolutely necessary. Before we can aspire to guide the destinies of India, we shall have to adopt the habit of fearlessness.

Gandhi showed the world a powerful model of sacrifice. He encouraged his own family and others who joined him in his ashrams to practice similar discipline. If Gandhi were to share a message about character today, he likely would say something about our need to develop more of a sacrificial spirit. He might address the importance of strong family ties. This was important to Gandhi, although he admitted many mistakes in raising his own children. He would acknowledge that continual learning is necessary, but point out that, in his judgment, the development of moral character must accompany formal education.

> "Strength in numbers is the delight of the timid. The valiant in spirit glory in fighting alone." —Gandhi

The caption on the cartoon reads "We have different weapons." To foreigners and particularly to the Westerners who had experienced the horrors of World War I, the most striking aspect of Gandhi's struggles for Indian independence was its use of peaceful, nonviolent means against the colossal, armed power of the British rulers. (1930)

Six

Worship Without Sacrifice

"Let no one for a moment entertain the fear that a reverent study of other religions is likely to weaken or to shake one's faith in one's own." —Gandhi

Gandhi perceived his role as a religious agent for change. The concept of religion without sacrifice as a social sin harmonized with his thinking. Having a deep belief in religion and in a personal, caring Creator, Gandhi was well aware of the failings of sinful actions done in the name of religion—as well as the essential greatness of those religions. In *Young India*, Gandhi wrote: "No doubt religion needs to answer for some of the most terrible crimes in history. But that is the fault not of religion, but of the ungovernable brute in man…"

Gandhi cherished all religions and refused to revile any of them. He chose to esteem each one because he viewed the major religions as different roads converging to the same point of worship. He believed that it was his duty, as indeed the duty of adherents of each time-tested religion, to help make necessary adjustments from their own individual conscience.

★★★

Gandhi's appreciation of religious teachings beyond his Hindu beliefs resonates with my Catholic perspective. My essay "Seeking to Live in Harmony" was published by in *The Post-Standard* as part of a series in which writers expressed their thoughts within a belief context.

> I believe with the psalmist that it is good to sing praise to God: 'To sing your love at dawn, your faithfulness at dusk.'
>
> I believe in the essential harmony of the universe, and that a supreme being, a marvelous Maestro, cares for each individual human being in the musical score of creation.
>
> I believe there is beauty and truth in all religions that have stood the test of time. While not subscribing to the idea that one religion is as good as another, I find the social teachings in the Hebrew and Christian scriptures, the Quran, the Vedas (Hindu Scriptures), and Buddhism to be in harmony with God's plan of creation.
>
> I believe in building up rather than tearing down. When Pope Benedict XVI approved the document in early July that compared other Christian denominations and religions with Catholicism, he once again showed his preference for criticizing rather than encouraging.
>
> For the other major religions of the world, it sounded a sour note. For other Christians, including Orthodox and Christian denominations, it was out of tune with an ecumenical spirit. Instead of singing the praises of the Catholic faith, he chose a different approach—one that seemed calculated to antagonize people of other religious beliefs.
>
> As a professor of mine once stated, "Comparisons are always odious." My own observation over a half-century has borne out the truth of that statement when it comes to judging others.
>
> I believe that today, America has too many prisoners in our federal state and local jails (more than 2,100,000). These mainly include men and women from racial and

ethnic minorities. As a nation founded on the ideals of liberty and justice, we can do better.

I believe that Jesus showed us the way to live our lives fully and truthfully. He taught us to love one another, even to love our enemies. Rather than condemning, Jesus gave us a very simple yardstick to measure others: "By their fruits, you shall know them!"

In harmony with nature, in harmony with our sisters and brothers everywhere, this, I believe, is a good way to live.

★★★

The Indian poet laureate Tagore conferred the name *Mahatma* (great soul) on Gandhi, and the village peasants and politicians in India gradually accepted it, although Gandhi never felt comfortable with its use. Throughout their public lives there was a mutual admiration between Tagore and Gandhi, close friends and contemporaries who chose different ways to address social problems. In 1919, after the passing of the Rowlett Act in India, a letter from Tagore to Gandhi pledged whole-hearted support and encouragement for his campaign to fight the legislation that allowed Indians to be arrested and imprisoned without legal recourse:

> We must know that moral conquest does not insist on success, that failure does not deprive it of its own ability and worth. Those who believe in the spiritual life know that to stand against the idea in the teeth of evident defeat.
>
> I have always felt and said accordingly that the great gift of freedom can never come to a person through charity. We must win it before we can own it. And India's opportunity for winning it will come to her when she can prove that she is morally superior to the people who rule her by their right of conquest. She must willingly accept her penance of suffering, which is the crown of the great. Armed with her utter faith in goodness, she must stand unabashed before the arrogance that scoffs at the power of spirit.

> And you come to your motherland in the time of her need to remind her of her mission, to lead her in the true path of conquest, to purge her present-day politics of the feebleness, which imagines that it has gained its purpose when it struts in the borrowed feathers of diplomatic dishonesty.

Previously Tagore had criticized Gandhi's effort to involve Indians in World War I, accusing him of compromising his principles. Gandhi was stung by the criticism that questioned his conviction to pacifism. Over time as Gandhi spread the concept of satyagraha in India, teaching it to his followers in various campaigns, he strengthened his friendship with Tagore, who, in turn, was willing to set aside his reservations about Gandhi's aborted war recruiting and resume good relations.

Tagore and Gandhi had similar spiritual outlooks. Gandhi embraced the spiritual everywhere he found it. As a Hindu he reached out to Muslims for reconciliation and harmony. He was opposed to political and religious division within his own country, and he fought to the very end against partition, the eventual separation of Pakistan from India, and its ensuing religious conflicts.

★★★

Gandhi's nonviolence had its roots back in childhood, but it seemed to solidify during his law training in England where he pursued his desire to be sustained in a prayerful, community setting, which explains his attraction to ashrams. His willingness to accept suffering became an intimate part of satyagraha movements and was connected to his religious beliefs. Religious students and theologians who later studied Gandhi's life saw the deep roots of his witness and how it was related to prayer life. One of Gandhi's later admirers, John Howard Yoder, a Mennonite theologian, came to the conclusion that "a life of sustained commitment to nonviolence against all odds is possible only if it rests on faith in God—in whom all human beings are one—and that faith is nurtured by a supportive, believing community."

Religious Reformer

When he saw the necessity, Gandhi was not hesitant to criticize fellow Indians or Hinduism. He espoused many parts of the Hindu religion, but grew increasingly critical of the caste system as he grew older. One of the reasons Gandhi embraced Hinduism, despite strongly criticizing some of its teachings, was that he found Hinduism to be very tolerant in scope of self-expression and fostering respect for other religions. Another reason was the Hindu principle of *swadeshi*, a compound term meaning loyalty to ones own region and the spirit attracting each person to his or her immediate surroundings, which Gandhi applied to religion as well: "By reason of the Swadeshi spirit, a Hindu refuses to change his religion, not necessarily because he considers it to be the best, but because he knows that he can complement it by introducing reforms." Gandhi called swadeshi the soul of self-rule. Thus, Gandhi continued to practice Hinduism and tried to purge defects he perceived within it. He encouraged people of other faiths to respect and honor the tenets of their own religious upbringing while persuasively working to purify and change teachings or traditions that one questions or rejects.

Gandhi worked relentlessly toward changing Hindu cultural and religious prohibitions on Untouchables. It was after returning to India that Gandhi took his stand against the Hindu caste system that labeled Untouchables. So strongly did Gandhi feel about the social outcasts in Indian society that he renamed Untouchables *harijans* (children of God) and named the last newspaper he founded *Harijan*. As Gandhi regarded their status an unnecessary excrescence to the Hindu faith, he developed his own theories on how the caste system should evolve. He was not opposed to the overall idea of caste, which is four thousand years old in India, although he always maintained that the concept of untouchability was repugnant to reason and to faith.

Even as a child Gandhi had intuited that there was something wrong with untouchability, telling his mother that he did not think it wrong to touch the "outcast" who came to their home to perform menial functions, even though his action violated Hindu religious law. After returning to India, Gandhi took a public stand against untouchablility. So deeply did he reject this religious and cultural discrimination—which affected nearly a fifth of the Hindu population—that the issue became a major focus of his life.

From the onset of their marriage, his wife was emotionally and culturally shaken by his position on equality for Untouchables. In the ashrams that Gandhi established in India, one basic rule for acceptance was the agreement that if any Untouchable individual or family applied they would be accepted as long as they were willing to abide by community rules. This came as a surprise to some of the community members at Sabarmati, Gandhi's first ashram in India, who were hostile to the idea. Most thought that no Untouchable individual or family would ever seek admission, so it appeared to be an academic issue. A critical point was reached when an Untouchable family with a young daughter, named Lakshmi, came to the ashram. This caused a rift and many, including Kasturba, were upset. This caused an argument between Gandhi and his wife, and was one of the few times when Gandhi lost his temper with her, which he later confessed with deep humiliation. For her part, Kasturba relented on this issue, and eventually came to appreciate his position, as did others in the ashram. Kasturba came to love Lakshmi and was saddened when the child eventually moved away with her family.

In 1932, Gandhi was concerned about impending legislation that he sensed would damage Untouchables and hinder their complete integration into the Hindu political process. His challenge was not only from those in higher castes, some Untouchables also strongly opposed Gandhi's position because they wanted separate representation. Gandhi was in prison at the time and declared that he would fast unto death unless the law included fair representation. The decision stirred the emotions of politicians and the populace into active concern for his well being. When Gandhi commenced the fast, Tagore shared this with the students in his school:

A shadow is darkened today over India like a shadow cast by an eclipsed sun. The people of the whole country are suffering from a poignant pain of anxiety, the universality of which carries in it a great dignity of consolation. Mahatmaji, who through his life of dedication, has made India his own in truth and has commenced his vow of extreme self-sacrifice.

Tagore, as a poet, articulated the anxious interest with which people from all corners of India, the government of Great Britain, and observers around the world followed the day-to-day progress of the fast, which Gandhi, at age sixty-three, began in an already weakened condition. Once it was underway, politicians scrambled to come up with a workable solution that was acceptable to the Untouchable leadership. Simultaneously, a dynamic change was sweeping across India as barriers restricting Untouchables from Hindu temples and public places were being removed on a daily basis. This sea change had near unanimous support from the people of India. Meanwhile, the nation waited to see if Gandhi would survive. It was a vibrant moment in the history of India. Six frantic days later, after a satisfactory agreement with all parties had been reached, Gandhi accepted his first orange juice.

Tagore endorsed the fast, saying, "No civilized society can thrive upon victims whose humanity has been permanently mutilated...those who we keep down invariably drag us down." Gandhi's single-minded fast provides an example of why the concept of religion without sacrifice resonated with him as a social sin.

Christianity

Gandhi had a strong attraction to Christianity and he often spoke positively about Christian services that he had attended. During times of recuperation from physical attacks and sickness he stayed in various Christian homes. Christians were members of his ashram communities and part of his social network.

He believed that there was a clear social dimension to worship, observing that prayer could lead a person to civil disobedience and non-cooperative satyagraha actions where the suffering experienced by the resisters might inspire a change of heart in the powerful, and that this shift could transform the world. In twice-daily prayer gatherings at his ashrams, the before-dawn and evening services, Gandhi frequently drew upon the teachings of Jesus as part of the communal prayer. He often requested the singing of Christian hymns and boasted that he could sing the refrain to "Lead Kindly Light" as well as any Christian. As a young man he considered converting to Christianity, but ultimately decided against it, and thereafter fully dedicated himself to Hinduism.

Gandhi said that the teachings of Jesus in the Sermon on the Mount[1] went straight to his heart, specifically Jesus' identification with the poor, the peacemakers, and those hurting in any way. He accepted the mandate of Jesus to love your enemies—the most difficult gospel challenge. This may well have been the inspiration for making nonviolence as fundamental to each of his social movements and as it was to his own lifestyle. Gandhi also deeply respected the willingness of Jesus to suffer and he encouraged his followers to be ready to do the same.

On more than one occasion Gandhi addressed conferences of Christian missionaries, sharing his perspective and praising their

---

[1] The Sermon on the Mount was Jesus' most famous sermon. (Mathew: 5-7) In it, he includes the Beatitudes, reconciling differences, loving your neighbor, giving, the Lord's Prayer, fasting, not worrying about money, food, clothing or tomorrow, not judging, and treating others as you want to be treated, among many other topics.

work; at the same time he let them know that he discouraged their proselytizing. The Hindu religion's refusal to actively encourage conversion was one of the features he appreciated most about it. Gandhi referred to himself as a humble student of religion. He only wished that Christians would live out the teachings of Jesus, not in fragments, but in a social way, rejecting violence on a personal and global scale. He urged the missionaries to live their life in such a way that their very life and actions would be the conduit to draw others toward Jesus' message.

Charles Andrews, Gandhi's trusted friend and confidant, was a man of deep Christian faith who helped Gandhi grow in appreciation for the New Testament teachings of Jesus, especially the Sermon on the Mount and the oneness of humanity. Gandhi studied the interactions of Jesus and the Pharisees in order to better serve the Untouchables. Terrence Rynne, author of *Gandhi and Jesus: The Saving Power of Nonviolence*, writes that Andrews realized "how deeply offended Christ was by racial and religious exclusiveness and how it called forth his severest condemnations;" an idea that influenced the lives of both Andrews and Gandhi. As the sole Christian member of Gandhi's inner circle, Andrews provided a strong witness that Gandhi admired.

Again and again, Gandhi's special regard for Jesus came out in his writings and in other ways. When biographer Louis Fischer spent a week with Gandhi in his ashram in 1942, the only piece of art in his mud hut was a black and white picture of Jesus. Tolstoy's *The Kingdom of God Is Within You* deeply moved Gandhi and influenced his spiritual journey. The heart of the book's message was belief in the power of love, the truth of nonviolence, and the fundamental teaching of Jesus, which opened up a new vision for Gandhi as a young man and shaped his life's outlook. Tolstoy's last novel *Resurrection* (1899) includes many of the issues that resonated with Gandhi: social reform, grasping ownership of private property, and liberation for women. In the novel, the main character, Nekhludov, rejects some of his inherited wealth and his materialistic lifestyle by sharing his land with the peasants who till it. The heroine in the story, Maslova, makes a complete break from prostitution, which had entrapped her, and in time she comes to a deep spirituality. Subtly emerging in the novel's conclusion is the nonviolent message of the Sermon on the Mount.

Over time, several Christian theologians have studied Gandhi's satyagraha movements, noting the efficacy of nonviolent action in actual practice. Rynne alludes to this connection:

> Focusing again on the life of Jesus, his nonviolent, pre-emptive forgiving way of living, leads us back to understanding that salvation is not just saving an individual for an afterlife. It is overcoming the domination system at work in this life—overcoming domination hierarchies, economic injustice, patriarchy, racism, ranking, and violence.

As Gandhi understood it, reciprocal willingness to listen to and respect the beliefs of one another is of vital importance for religious leaders and followers. While difficult at times, such openness can help to address and undercut the roots of violence in our world. Healing comes slowly, but is possible. Gandhi was always tolerant. He saw truth in every religion and understood that whatever flaws seemed to exist in each were usually caused by people who misinterpreted certain teachings.

Noncooperation

Gandhi viewed the various organizational movements that he inspired as primarily religious, even though they were often very political in their thrust. Noncooperation was one of them and the concept extended to many dimensions of Indian life: wearing foreign clothing, payment of taxes, military service, and government employment.

In India, noncooperation began under Gandhi's leadership in 1920 after it became evident that Britain was taking a hard line on the nation's move toward self-government. The first national satyagraha action that Gandhi undertook in India was a response to the Rowlatt Act, which had been passed by the viceroy's legislature in Delhi. The Rowlatt Act severely restricted the rights of Indians to participate in political activity. In effect, it declared martial law, allowing Indians to be kept in prison without trial. Gandhi had fought against this legislation for months, and once it passed Gandhi pondered ways to respond. The idea of a *hartal* (general strike) came to him in a dream. The hartal would suspend economic activity for a day in which people would focus their energy on concomitant prayer and fasting. The idea spread rapidly and energized the population. The idea of noncooperation with British authorities was approved at the annual meeting of the Indian Congress. It was a dramatic and chaotic time. When the next Congressional session convened a year later, 20,000 Indians had already been jailed for civil disobedience.

Throughout 1921, Gandhi met six times with the British viceroy, Lord Reading, the newly appointed administrative leader of India. In these sessions, Gandhi stressed his nonviolent movement, carefully putting it in a religious context. Placing the task of purifying India as the first step towards swaraj, Gandhi believed independence from Britain would follow naturally. Lord Reading, in a letter to his son, later expressed a deep admiration for Gandhi. While the viceroy mentioned that there was nothing unusual about Gandhi's appearance, his description of Mahatma's speech is noteworthy:

He is direct and expresses himself well in excellent English with a fine appreciation in the value of the words he uses. There is no hesitation about him, and there is a ring of sincerity in all that he utters…and he is convinced to a point almost bordering on fanaticism that nonviolence and love will give India its independence and enable it to withstand the British government.

In the early months of 1922, rather than begin a mass movement of civil disobedience across India at once, Gandhi targeted a limited area, composed of 137 small villages with a population of fewer than 100,000 residents. His intention was to reveal the movement's power to completely paralyze the British ability to enforce laws. The demonstration never took place—called off by Gandhi—because of violence against the British elsewhere in India. The sudden termination of the action was an unpopular decision, but Gandhi stuck with it, insisting that the movement proceed only in a nonviolent way. He then fasted for five days to become a fitter instrument for leadership in these critical decisions.

As Gandhi's first political act in India against the British government, it was successful beyond anyone's imagination, despite the frustration by many at its cancellation. Gandhi wanted everyone participating to understand the importance of nonviolence. A core group of people, who had trained with Gandhi at his ashrams, either went to jail or spread out to villages and cities across India to share the message of satyagraha. Among these followers, Gandhi insisted on ahimsa. In this first hartal, he had learned the lesson that unless protest organizers were converted to the philosophy of satyagraha, strong emotions could lead to violence that might easily get out of hand. Overall, his first public actions in India gave citizens a new sense of power and pride, and Gandhi became an esteemed leader—their mahatma. This was the beginning of the long struggle against the British government, before independence was eventually granted in 1947.

While Gandhi originally respected the rule of British law and defended it publicly, he eventually saw its unequal and negative consequences for the Indian people. His response was to encourage noncooperation in serious ways, such as participation in the general strike. His noncooperation movement, when enjoined by public opinion and support from rank-and-file villagers, stymied British officials. Once the Indian population generally accepted this approach, it became part of their political power. Gandhi wrote, "Noncooperation is not a movement of brag, bluster, or bluff. It is a test of our sincerity. It requires solid and silent self-sacrifice. It challenges our honesty and our capacity for national work. It is a movement that aims at translating ideas into action. And the more we do, the more we find that much more must be done than we had expected."

El Salvador

One individual who took to heart the connection between worship and sacrifice was the former archbishop of El Salvador, Oscar Romero. Romero had been a conservative priest for much of his life, but after seeing a fellow priest and friend murdered in 1977 because of his work organizing poor farmers, he became more radical. He brought attention to the human rights abuses taking place in El Salvador and called for the United States to halt aid, which, under president Carter it did not choose to do. Neither did the Vatican support his campaign to address torture and poverty.

Romero was murdered in 1980. The previous day he had broadcast a plea on the radio asking the soldiers of El Salvador to refrain from violence and, if necessary, to disobey orders to shoot fellow citizens - who were sometimes literally their own brothers and sisters. Romero was shot while celebrating Mass; his death was later traced to an order from S.O.A. graduate Roberto D'Aubuisson. The reaction to his death in Latin America was dramatic. He had become a living example of liberation theology by embracing the struggle of the poor in his country and by challenging repressive government actions. Like the assassination of Gandhi, news of Romero's death resounded throughout the world.

Romero remains a hero and a martyr in Central America. His picture can be found in many of the poorest dwellings. Although he perceived that he was being targeted, he refused to be silent. He said that they could kill him, but that he would rise again in the people of his country. Excerpts from a prayer he shared, which was originally from a homily by Cardinal John Deardon, explains his perspective at the time of his death:

> We accomplish in our lifetime only a tiny fraction
> of the magnificent enterprise that is God's work.
> Nothing we do is complete, which is another way of saying
> that the Kingdom always lies beyond us...
> We cannot do everything, and there is a sense of liberation

in realizing that. This enables us to do something and to do it very well. It may be incomplete, but it is a beginning, a step along the way, an opportunity for the Lord's grace to enter and do the rest.

We may never see the end results, but that is the difference between the master builder and the worker.

We are workers, not master builders; ministers, not messiahs. We are prophets of a future that is not our own.

Toward the end of his life, Gandhi had the same premonition that Romero later experienced. After the separation of Pakistan from India, the emotions and feelings between Muslims and Hindus reached a fever pitch. Gandhi discerned that he might be killed because of his efforts to bring them together. He was quoted as saying he hoped he would have the courage to forgive any person who would kill him. In January 1948, a Hindu fanatic, upset at Gandhi's support for the Muslims, shot Gandhi at close range.

★★★

As part of a memorial ecumenical service for Archbishop Romero ten years after his death, I shared a poem I'd written:

El Salvador

The Savior!
Tucked away in a tiny corner of the world, a prophetic naming.
For innocent blood has flowed over her soil like a wellspring from an open tap.
Some thirteen thousand dead or missing at last count.
Early last year, Archbishop Romero's plea to President Carter:
"Don't send arms!"
Romero gunned down at the altar a few days later.
U.S. sends arms.

Late last year, four American missionary women killed.
U.S. halts arms.
An investigation is promised by the "ruling Junta."
U.S. resumes arms shipments.
Other nations refuse to send arms—West Germany—Britain—Japan.
Other missionaries echo the archbishop's anguish: "—don't send weapons to those killing   the common people."
But we send arms.
Our investments are important "in our backyard," and Cuba is "up to something."
Now it's military advisors. Looks like fifty or so will be enough!
No troops, just arms.
And the blood keeps flowing as Lent continues…
…send for water to wash our hands, again.

Romero led by example and inspired. On the 25th anniversary of his martyrdom in 2005, his courage motivated me to participate in civil disobedience at the gates of the School of the Americas.

Seamless Garment

Although Gandhi at times perceived that the fruits of his labor seemed to be drying up, he could not have known to what extent his ideas were spreading throughout the world. One example can be seen in South Africa, many years after the birth of satyagraha, as Nelson Mandela and Anglican Archbishop Desmond Tutu led their country toward reconciliation after a long period of violence and repression. Tutu, like Gandhi, was not afraid to step between factions of an angry crowd at critical times. An example of this occurred at the funeral of slain civil rights leader Stephen Biko, when the mood of a large assembly was volatile with sorrow and barely contained anger. Tutu spoke about forgiveness, exhorting the mourners to remain nonviolent. In that instance, as in others in South Africa, the spirit of reconciliation prevailed over violent retaliation. Tutu humbly acknowledges that he becomes very uncomfortable when compared to Gandhi, but he readily admits his influence on him.

Fourteen years after Gandhi's death, Tutu, like Gandhi before him, went to England to study. On his return to South Africa, Tutu began preaching liberation theology, calling on people to oppose oppression, injustice, and corruption. At the same time, he demonstrated his resistance through public actions. He called politics and religion a "seamless garment," refusing the idea that there is any difference between the two realms.

The seamless garment metaphor has relevance from a nonviolent perspective. The idea that every act of violence is to be rejected and eschewed was a value that Gandhi taught and lived. This concept has been applied to many current moral issues, including debates on abortion, racism, the death penalty, and euthanasia among others. The seamless garment approach would include a nonviolent approach as part of each discussion. While Gandhi did not use the term seamless garment, we can only surmise that he would have endorsed this concept.

Gandhi always respected his adversaries. While he disagreed with their positions he would listen to their arguments patiently, but he stuck to his principles. He never insisted that his adversaries agree with him, and he carefully avoided expressions of anger or hatred toward them. Instead, he respected them and tried to form relationships with them, even while remaining in disagreement. If he deemed a decision would be detrimental to the process of moving India in the best direction, he would concede. He had no ego in matters of politics or anything else. Even in the ashrams, he was quite open to listening to members who disagreed with him on different matters, yet on issues like untouchability, he was steadfast. His inclusion of Untouchables was a solid rule in his ashrams and underscored his belief in the dignity and rights of every human being. In this area too, the analogy of a seamless garment would seem to fit Gandhi's thinking.

Another example from Gandhi's life illustrates his open-mindedness. In January 1936, when he was sixty-six, he was visited by an American, Margaret Sanger. Her personal mission was to bring birth control to India, and she sought Gandhi's approval for this enterprise. Sanger arrived on a Monday, and at that time in Gandhi's life, it was his day of silence. Ten years earlier, at the age of fifty-six, after a year of extensive traveling and speaking, Gandhi adopted a day of silence for himself each week. From that point on, he only spoke on a Monday if there was a pressing need. He felt silent days helped him become a better listener, clarified his thinking and improved his arguments regardless of the subject or issue of the moment. When Sanger arrived, the two of them smiled and greeted one another in silence, but had no discussion until the following day. On Tuesday, they began an animated discussion that lasted several days. In this case, while he agreed on the need for birth control and population control, his idea of the way to accomplish it was in contrast to Sanger's approach, since he was opposed to any artificial means. After considerable time discussing the issue quite intensely, they parted without either changing the other's mind.

When Fischer spent a week with Gandhi in his ashram in 1942, he asked him about the origin of silent Mondays. Gandhi admitted that there was no great spiritual driving force behind them; after traveling extensively and feeling torn and frazzled, he felt the need to rest, and being silent one day a week was his chosen method. He joked that he later cloaked it with all kinds of virtue, but it was nothing of the kind, just a day of personal reflection and rest. Gandhi was, above all, an honest man.

In today's discussions about sensitive moral issues with political overtones, similar periods of silent reflection might be beneficial for proponents of opposing positions. For example, careful thought while listening to differing views on abortion have helped some individuals and groups see common threads and better appreciate one another's viewpoint, even though disagreements remain. Most can agree on renewed efforts to protect the lives of newborns and of children at every stage of growth. Almost everyone on both sides of the debate dislikes abortion and looks for ways to lessen their number. They often have different ideas about achieving this goal, and religious issues are often at the forefront of these many-sided discussions. Advocates on both sides of the abortion issue have been willing to sacrifice for their beliefs. Women who have faced the difficult issue in their own personal lives have often made great sacrifices.

It is difficult to separate political and moral issues. Gandhi made no distinction. Judging from Gandhi's position on birth control, it's safe to assume that he would oppose abortion, though his thinking on the matter was not evident. If the issue had come up when he was participating in the Indian Congress, it would be interesting to know how he would have addressed it. We do know that he worked for women's rights in Hindu society and was considered by many to be their champion. Women joined him in all the satyagraha movements and many went to jail after engaging in civil disobedience.

★★★

In a letter published on September 25, 2008 in *The Catholic Sun*, I addressed the issue of abortion from the political perspective, especially during presidential elections.

> Every four years, at presidential election time, letters to the editor appear in this paper, urging Catholics to vote for candidates who describe themselves as "pro-life." This trend seems especially true when a Catholic politician is

running on the Democratic ticket, as in this year. Abortion is their focus issue.

As in the past, when those who profess to be "pro-life" are elected, nothing seems to change one way or the other on the national scene. This is partly true because rank and file constituents, both Republican and Democrat, are about equally divided on the abortion issue and how best to approach it. Most people in both major political parties want to see a significant reduction in abortions. This goal will only be achieved when the issue is viewed in a broader sense than the perspective of one Supreme Court decision. Were Roe vs. Wade to be overturned, the issue would return to each state for a political decision. Even then, if abortion was ruled illegal in some or all states, abortions would continue.

The ultimate decision to bring a child into this world is a personal, private, and religious one, often joyful. Thoughtful reflections, aided by progressive social programs, would allow mothers and fathers to know that they can raise their children to be healthy adults. Meaningful jobs, health care, and education are critical. Minimum wages also need to be sufficient to allow families to function well.

Our support should be for the candidates who we think will best promote the common good.

This is our best hope for a reduction of abortions in the near future.

In a different seamless garment realm, but one that is also emotionally charged, is the issue of the death penalty. In New York state, because of vigils, legal challenges, and other political actions, the State Assembly has put enforcement of the death penalty on hold. Other states, as well as a few countries, still utilize capitol punishment, often basing their arguments on the assumption of deterrence. Where the death penalty exists there is always resistance from groups of citizens opposed to the government taking a life. In the case of Gandhi, his murderer was later subjected to the death penalty, much to the dismay and opposition of many of Gandhi's followers who felt that his belief in ahimsa was not honored.

The seamless garment concept also applies to the question of participating in war. Some theologians find it impossible to conceive of reasons for nations to go to war in this nuclear age; others disagree. Even advocates for the total abolishment of full-scale war understand that military peacekeeping is sometimes necessary.

Judaism

One of the most difficult moral issues in Gandhi's time was the rise of Hitler and the Third Reich. At this point in his life, Gandhi had become completely convinced of the power and efficacy of carrying nonviolence in one's heart, even in facing a tyrant like Hitler. Here are some of Gandhi's thoughts framed in a religious context:

> My sympathies are all with the Jews. They have been the untouchables of Christianity… The parallel between their treatment by Christians and the treatment of untouchables by Hindus is very close. Religious sanction has been invoked in both cases for the justification of the inhuman treatment meted out to them…But the German persecution of the Jews seems to have no parallel in history.

Gandhi believed that the Jews in Germany were in a stronger position, intellectually, to offer satyagraha resistance than the Indians in South Africa. He had come to a complete pacifist position, and even though he realized the terrible plight of the Jewish people in Germany at that time, he encouraged a response that was based on maintaining dignity and refusing to fight back.

In this thinking, as in other controversial positions, many disagreed with Gandhi's idealism. Yet, we can see in it the depth of his appreciation of nonviolence and the power that he attributed to individuals who were committed to it, even to the extent of giving up of their lives. This, he himself, was willing to do when entering into a satyagraha action or taking on a fast. In his thoughts about Jewish resistance in 1938, we can discern some of Gandhi's ideas about war, including his complete personal rejection of it. Nonviolence had come to be an absolute principle in his own life, even as he recognized that he could not dictate his conclusions to his friends in the Indian Congress, close associates, or the young Indian men of military age. This was part of his evolution of thought on the subject.

★★★

While I was incarcerated, a friend sent me a copy of *Constantine's Sword: The Church and the Jews* by James Carroll. The book carefully traces through many centuries the unfolding of the Christian and Jewish experiences in relation to one another, beginning with Jesus and Paul, both Jews. Through careful scholarship laced with personal experience, Carroll presents insights into the traditional enmity between the religions, along with missed opportunities for mutual understanding and respect.

Christians have had the upper hand from the time of the Roman Emperor Constantine (AD 306-337) when they endeavored to meld Christianity and empire. The results were often unfavorable to Jews, most notably with the establishment of the Inquisition (Middle Ages -19th century), the pogroms in Russia, and the Jewish ghettoes and concentration camps of the Holocaust.

The historical struggle between Jews and Christians has fluctuated in various times and places. Biased language in the Catholic liturgy reflects this history. Pope John XXIII (1958-1963) began to address this issue by eliminating derogatory statements from the Good Friday service. Some Vatican II developments, especially the document on Religious Freedom, encouraged genuine tolerance in the Catholic community. Unfortunately, a 2007 papal document gave permission to return to the Tridentine liturgy and renewed the controversy, as it allows the option to once again include offensive prayer language. The lack of understanding and respect between Christians and Jews throughout the centuries underscores Gandhi's perspective on how religious suspicions and ignorance can be an underlying cause of violence.

Worship and Sacrifice in Prison

The population of Canaan Federal Prison Camp in 2006 was relatively stable at one hundred and sixty male inmates. Within that number, there was a great range of religious faiths and approaches to worship. Informal, often spontaneous, prayer gatherings were more evident than scheduled ones. Formal services were offered mainly by three chaplains on staff—all white, Protestant, and male. They appeared to come from similar religious and cultural backgrounds, but I attended only one of their fundamentalist services, so I have little firsthand knowledge of their spirit or content. Feedback about them from other inmates, however, gave me the impression that these services seemed to call for little sacrifice beyond acceptance of our incarcerated situation and, as always, a call to an individual relationship with Jesus. Outside of the chaplains' minimal counseling hours and a weekly scheduled prayer service, there was only one other formal religious offering. A priest from a neighboring parish celebrated a Catholic mass on most Thursday afternoons.

The informal gatherings, on the other hand, gave indication of real diversity. A Native American sweat lodge brought a few inmates together each week. These were heavily regulated by the prison staff - when a new inmate attended one of these sessions and missed a work assignment, mistakenly thinking he had permission from a chaplain to attend, he was punished for several weeks in the segregated housing unit (SHU). There were also daily prayer gatherings of Christian inmates, mostly African Americans, who came together for five to ten minutes of common prayer before supper. The timing meant they often missed mail call—an event to which many inmates looked forward. More importantly, these inmates participated in an effort to welcome new inmates with a care package and informally tried to orient them to their new surroundings. This called for a sacrifice of their time and meager material goods in order to share with newcomers.

A dozen Muslim inmates prayed individually, and at times collectively, without an imam to lead them. Several prayed five times daily, facing the east, and when time allowed kneeling on individual prayer rugs alongside their bunks. Early each morning, a few would gather together in prayer well before the 6 A.M. wake-up call. Most, if not all, were Sunni, as a young Muslim informed me. He was on a religious, vegetarian-meal plan, and sometimes offered me the whole wheat bread from his tray. Muslim inmates seemed to fit in well with the general population. I witnessed no proselytizing and no animosity between Muslims and other inmates.

There were a handful of Jewish inmates. A few of them carried out Shabbat services, without a rabbi, every Friday evening. The inmate leader was Russian born, with an extraordinary singing voice that rivaled any cantor I have ever heard. Russ, as his friends called him, prayed daily in the chapel room, draping a prayer shawl around his shoulders. He was an avid student of the Torah, and he worked constantly on his Hebrew pronunciation. In addition, he was the finest chess player in the camp, voluntarily leading a weekly chess class that attracted many inmates and helped them socialize and practice some mental skills.

The faithfulness of the Jews to the covenant of Abraham and Moses and a continuing appreciation of God's creation came through to me when I attended Shabbat service on Friday evenings. Each participant took turns reading one or more of the psalms. It felt comfortable to integrate my own Catholic faith as I reacquainted myself with the Hebrew psalms. After we finished the service with the symbolic matzos and grape juice, we shared some of the similarities and differences of our respective beliefs. We discussed many common scriptural texts as well as some of the tensions between our religions that have persisted through the centuries.

A personal interaction involving one of the Jewish inmates happened during my first week of incarceration. It was also Holy Week for Christians. When at breakfast that Friday, I placed only a small amount of food on my tray. He asked me why I wasn't eating more. I replied, "It's Good Friday." With a disarming smile, he responded, "I hope so!"

Sometimes, it takes a piece of art to illustrate stark differences in various positions. The cartoon (page 94) showing Gandhi in front of a huge, imposing war tank captures such a contrast. The caption "We have different weapons" makes a powerful point. Gandhi's weapon was nonviolent resistance. When faced with civil resistance of this sort, the might of the British Empire was forced to reconsider its position. What would Gandhi say about war to the United States today? The fact that our country has a military budget larger than the combined total of all the other military budgets in the world would certainly be addressed.

Within the context of worship without sacrifice, Gandhi might certainly urge more religious tolerance, inviting us to take time to learn about the religious faiths of our neighbors in order to celebrate religious diversity. Gandhi might tell us to make prayer a part of each day and to pray and worship within a supportive community. In Gandhi's good-humored way, he would share his perception that religion should never be glum, and if you find it that way, change it! Perhaps Gandhi would encourage young and old to be peacemakers and draw our attention to Jesus' teachings in the Sermon on the Mount.

> "The only people on Earth who do not see Christ and his teachings as nonviolent are Christians." —Gandhi

Danger Signal

As negotiations on the transfer of power continued through the early part of 1947, it became increasingly evident that partition of the country was seemingly inevitable. On May 6, in a last effort to change the course of history, Gandhi met Mohammad Ali Jinnah in New Delhi. The meeting was friendly he said later, but Jinnah was "quite firm that the question of Pakistan was not open to discussion." Gandhi is shown here hoisting a danger signal to prevent India, a train, from derailing—as the track points in divergent directions. (1947)

Seven

Politics Without Principle

"I believe that it is possible to introduce uncompromising truth and honesty in the political life of the country...I would strain every nerve to make Truth and Nonviolence accepted in all our national activities. Then, we should cease to fear or distrust our governments and their measures." —Gandhi

Gandhi did not seek out a political role for himself. His initial participation in the Indian National Congress was on a voluntary basis. He tells us in his autobiography that, in 1919, he tried to leave the Congress, but was prevailed upon to stay. He accepted a leadership role because British laws were becoming intolerable to the Indian population; soldiers under the command of Brigadier General Reginald Dyer had carried out a massacre. The Rowlatt Act, passed by the Imperial Legislation Council in Delhi, in March 1918, extended "severe emergency war powers" to the British. While Gandhi participated in the debate over it, he afterwards considered it to be a farcical legal formality. The oppressive law had been passed because the majority of the voting members were British government officials. Any Indian accused of sedition could be tried without a jury with no opportunity to appeal. The mere possession of printed material deemed threatening to the government could bring a prison sentence of two years.

Once in a position of influence, Gandhi maneuvered to open the All-Indian Congress to rank-and-file members from around the country. Encouraged by Gandhi, people from villages, towns and cities accepted the invitation. In 1919, about 7,000 delegates attended the annual political convention in central India. The following year over 20,000 people attended. If there was a single political principle that Gandhi practiced, it was his effort to include everyone who was willing and capable of participating in the process. He accepted a leadership role in the Congress, but refused to engage in any partisan or divisive action.

Martin Luther King Jr.'s Tribute

In the United States, the civil rights movement was inspired by Gandhi's principles, with so many people peacefully risking arrest in order to state their concerns before a court. All were willing to accept jail sentences. The entire U.S. civil rights movement owes a debt to Gandhi, as Martin Luther King Jr. never tired of acknowledging. In 1959, before he became recognized as a civil rights leader, King spent a month touring India, examining the results of Gandhi's civil disobedience campaigns. On the 50th anniversary of his visit, a recently discovered voice recording of King's message to the Indian people reveals the visit's impact on him. King came to understand that Gandhi's "method of nonviolent resistance is the most potent weapon available to oppressed people in their struggle for justice and human dignity," and he claimed that "Mahatma Gandhi embodied in his life certain universal principles that are inherent in the moral structure of the universe."

In the recording, King compared Gandhi to Abraham Lincoln, both of whom were shot "trying to heal the wounds of a divided nation" and both of whom now "belong to the ages." King also said:

> If this age is to survive, it must follow the way of love and nonviolence that he so nobly illustrated in his life. And Mahatma Gandhi may well be God's appeal to this generation. On a day when sputniks and explorers dash through outer space and guided by ballistic missiles that carve highways of death through the stratosphere, no nation can win a war. Today, we no longer have a choice between violence and nonviolence. It is either nonviolence or nonexistence.

Throughout the world today, many, perhaps most, groups and individuals opposing war, violence and repressive governments pattern their resistance on Gandhian principles. In the U.S., civil disobedience has played a significant role in civil rights and anti-war movements since in the 1960s. Activists opposing wars in Vietnam, Iraq, Afghanistan and elsewhere have been largely focused on nonviolent witness using Gandhian methods. Occasionally, but very rarely, some individuals, who lack training and discipline in nonviolence, will resist arrest. In large-scale actions, some violence occasionally breaks out. When such outbreaks occurred in Gandhi's time, it always saddened him and at times he stopped the action, even if it appeared to be achieving success.

Bridging Hindu-Muslim Tensions

Gandhi looked for inspiration from God in his communal prayer life and in his dreams. His fellow Indians never questioned his deep belief in a creative, personal God. The prayers at his ashrams included readings and hymns from different religious faiths. Having an abiding belief in all time-tested religions, Gandhi understood that part of his life's work was to heal the cultural, religious, and emotional rift between Muslims and Hindus. He pursued this effort so that members of these two faiths might live peacefully with each other, while still holding to their own set of beliefs. He had many Muslim friends, and he went out of his way to invite them to his ashrams and to visit their homes. He credited Islam for bringing the firm belief in Allah, the One God, into the Hindu mind and heart, replacing much of Hindu's polytheism. He also criticized aspects of Islam, as he did of his own Hindu religion. In the case of Islam, Gandhi objected to the readiness of some Muslims to choose the sword over nonviolent discussion and to sometimes force conversion on unwilling Hindu believers.

Gandhi recognized the potential tragedy of inflaming the passions of Hindus and Muslims in India. In the villages, members of these two groups had lived together in peace. Tensions between them arose in dense urban areas, when both poverty and oppressive weather conditions made daily life difficult. When violence occurred it was vicious. Gandhi was discouraged by attitudes of bickering and hatred among both Hindus and Muslims. Intense fighting in 1924 prompted Gandhi to undertake a twenty-one day water-only fast for Hindu-Muslim friendship at the home of a his friend, Mohammad Ali, a Muslim, staunch Indian Congress supporter and believer in Hindu-Muslim unity. As Gandhi's condition deteriorated, on the twelfth day of the fast, he wrote:

> Hitherto, it has been a struggle and a change of heart among Englishmen who compose the government of India. That change has still to come. But the struggle must

for the moment be transferred to a change of heart among the Hindus and the Mussulmans. Before they dare think of freedom, they must be brave enough to love one another, to tolerate one another's religion, even prejudices, and superstitions, and to trust one another. This requires faith in oneself. And faith in oneself is faith in God. If we have faith, we shall cease to fear one another."

His heroic effort threatened his life; it also stopped the violence.

Gandhi tried to perform his actions so simply that even the humblest of individuals could understand. Even beyond desire for understanding, however, his witness was never given to humiliate an opponent, but to heal and encourage. Gandhi respected justice, and even during his own political trials, he lectured judges on their responsibility in this regard. This fundamental justice principle of Gandhi's was faithfully exercised in his individual relationships as well as in the collective political process. The fact that millions of people in small villages and rural areas throughout India came to know and appreciate Gandhi and his message speak highly of the power of the man and those principles. The poor peasants of India came to endorse and wholeheartedly embrace him as the Mahatma.

Jubilee Justice

The way in which ordinary Indian villagers and city dwellers came to revere and follow Gandhi reflects, to a degree, the way the Israelites followed Moses, as we know from the Hebrew Scriptures. Moses was the great lawgiver of the Israelites. He did not choose the role of politician, yet, in a sense, that position was thrust upon him. He tried to negotiate with the pharaoh in Egypt, he tried to steady his constituents during their long trek in the wilderness, and he argued for his people when he thought Yahweh was displeased with them. Moses also put into place laws that he judged to be in the best interests of the Hebrew people under his jurisdiction. Gandhi similarly accepted his role in political life. While he was a single member of the Indian Congress, others looked to him for leadership when decisions needed to be made.

Within the context of laws developed for the Israelites under Moses' leadership were several directives steeped in moral principles that came to be understood as "jubilee." These included a farsighted plan in which elements of care for the land, forgiveness of debt, freeing of servants or slaves, and a continual connection with family roots were each prescribed under certain conditions and at certain intervals. There are social and political dimensions to these jubilee regulations, carefully spelled out in the books of Leviticus and Exodus. Underlying the entire concept is the principle of justice. Jubilee means a sense of letting go, a time for making amends, and respect for the earth: all basic justice issues.

Gandhi was deeply concerned about issues of justice and food security for the multitudes of Indian peasants scattered in small communities throughout the country. Most had such a small patch of land that they were unable to grow enough food for their families. Many were exploited when they tried to borrow money. Millions were completely impoverished. Deaths from famine in India in the 19th century numbered more than twenty-one million. To put this in context, the population of India in 1800 was 140 million, in 1900 it was 234 million.

Mediation

One important dimension of the jubilee construct found in Hebrew Scriptures is forgiveness. There is always a need to establish a time for forgiveness and reconciliation, and sometimes, restorative justice, whether weekly, yearly, in a sabbatical seventh year, or during a jubilee forty-ninth year. When Gandhi practiced law in South Africa and when he himself was on trial in India, he encouraged and used mediation whenever possible.

Shortly after Gandhi established his first ashram in India, across the Sabarmati River from the industrial city of Ahmadabad, a strike was initiated by nearby textile workers in response to wages at the mills where they worked. Even though he was a friend of the mill owners, Gandhi took the side of labor when the strike began. He was able to convince the workers to carry out their strike in a nonviolent way using satyagraha. Daily, he worked with the workers on strategy. When they were discouraged, he initiated a fast to give them encouragement. Eventually the textile workers were able to convince the mill owners to agree to a new contract. In this instance, and thereafter, Gandhi's aim was conciliation and mediation. Through it all, he remained friends with the mill owners, even as he ensured the workers' grievances were heard and their demands addressed.

The art of mediation and reconciliation was a hallmark of Gandhi's efforts and it helped break vicious cycles of rage and pervasive fears. When those in power feed upon these emotions, they surrender the moral high ground of justice. When perceiving that ethical principles were being violated, Gandhi fought to bring them to light. In his newspapers, he publicized letters from people who opposed him or disagreed with his positions. Human relationships for Gandhi were of critical importance. Rejecting a cynical outlook, he kept a positive view of political power. He had not chosen to be a politician, and he was pleased when he no longer had a formal role in the Indian Congress. Nonetheless, he continued to advise politicians who sought his counsel. Gandhi's opinions were given great weight, and he was often chosen as a spokesperson at high-level conferences.

Gandhi realized that politics can twist the concept of justice in devious ways. When this happened, he fought such decisions, but not against lawmakers themselves. In the cases of the Black Act in South Africa and the Rowlatt Act in India, Gandhi organized to oppose the legislation while connecting humanly with the lawmakers. His satyagraha movements were severely tested, since they involved civil rights issues with strong opposition from powerful opponents, but satyagraha succeeded in both cases.

Key and Bolt

A studied attempt to imitate the nonviolent teaching in the Sermon on the Mount was a challenge Gandhi accepted. He prayed daily for the strength to live the beatitudes and other lessons from Jesus' life. Ashram members gathered in the early morning and at the end of the day to pray and sing. These times were at the heart of community life for Gandhi; he referred to them as the key in the morning and the bolt in the evening.

Since Gandhi's time, individuals engaging in nonviolent actions have been documented throughout the world. Multitudes have never been documented. Many mirror in a small way the vitriol Gandhi faced again and again in South Africa and India. His family members often endured the same enmity. Gandhi continually rose above such personal attacks, modeling a positive response to Jesus' challenging ideas and exacting life witness. His communal prayer life provided an anchor for his decisions and actions. Even though these struggles were intense, calling as they did for great self-sacrifice, he modeled for his followers respect for his opponents. Sometimes, he went out of his way to show respect for his foes, even when it wasn't appreciated. At fifty-five, Gandhi was able to say: "By a long process of prayerful discipline, I have ceased for over forty years to hate anybody. I know that this is a big claim…but I can and do hate evil wherever it exists."

Gandhi named his first permanent ashram in India Satyagraha Ashram. It was the truth-force concept of action, with its underlying belief in the power of ahimsa, that attracted members. In difficult and tense situations involving large gatherings, Gandhi dispersed his close followers, especially those trained in his ashrams, to the volatile sites. Some demonstrations, like the hartal, involved millions. Once it became a nationwide strike, his team members were limited in their influence and it was up to the people of India to live as satyagrahis.

Judicial Discretion

During three months in prison, I got to know several inmates who were serving long sentences for nonviolent offenses. My own observation, along with those of fellow prisoners in the minimum-security facility, was that at least half of the inmates there could easily be handled in a parole setting, if it was granted in their home community. In such an arrangement, even while reporting to a parole officer they would be able to maintain a job and help support their families.

When it came to spending time in prison, Gandhi was an exception. Because of the pressure that he often felt from his decisions to plan and engage in satyagraha actions, when arrested he often experienced a sense of relief. Gandhi made light of his prison time, saying that it provided respite from the stress of various movement struggles. He read, he wrote, he spun, and he worked. Yet, he also understood how difficult prison was for so many others in the movement—men and women who sacrificed their freedom in the struggle for justice, and often caused sacrifices within their families as well.

One example of a prisoner at Canaan weighed down by family issues was Michael, a middle-aged, pleasant individual with an Italian surname. He did not dispute the fact that he had broken the law by engaging in financial misdeeds at work that involved a fair sum of money, but the total amount was miniscule compared to recent revelations of embezzlement on Wall Street. The source of his anger was not the fact of his imprisonment but the length of his sentence and the effect it was having on his family relationships.

When he heard that the Pope was giving an honor to the judge who had presided over his case, he wrote to the Vatican. One Thursday, a visiting young priest arrived to celebrate the weekly liturgy and brought Michael a response from the Vatican as well as privately spoke with him after the service. Michael was informed that no retraction of the award was forthcoming; nevertheless he was surprised and grateful that the Pope or someone reasonably close to him had received his message and responded.

The judge had sentenced Michael to eighty-five months, more time than the federal guidelines suggested. Michael thought that the fact that he could never return to his profession, together with the needs of his wife and young children, should have warranted a reduced sentence. The stress on his family had been such that he wondered about his future relationship with them. Michael believes in his case the judge could and should have used his discretion. He feels he was treated unjustly.

In light of Michael's sentence, consider an observation by Chris Hedges, the author of *Losing Moses on the Freeway*. In this book, Hedges, a former newspaper reporter and war correspondent, takes a different slant on each of the Ten Commandments given to Moses. In the chapter on theft, the seventh commandment, Hedges focuses on a former stockbroker who became a reporter and had a successful career with *The Wall Street Journal*. This stockbroker, failing to disclose a conflict of interest, got caught in a scheme of deception and served a short prison term. Hedges noted that, "the crime he committed was a small infraction, but a symptom of the deep ethical and moral morass within the American culture."

A decade ago, a federal law was passed which allowed the stock market to monitor itself. Federal Reserve Chairman Alan Greenspan advocated, over two decades, for the idea of libertarian deregulation, and he succeeded in changing the structure of checks and balances in the financial system. Regulatory agencies, which monitored market activities, were eliminated. With this opening, according to Hedges, greed moved to the fore. "CEOs of companies helped themselves to hundreds of millions of dollars, as their small investors were wiped out," he writes, "Nearly all of the top Enron executives, despite amassing fortunes in the hundreds of millions of dollars, have avoided prison or huge fines."

New awareness of the greed exhibited by many within the financial system occurred in 2008, when toxic assets caused the "bubble to burst" on the housing market. Lack of regulations led speculators into new financial territory, as subprime mortgage schemes brought riches to some in the industry, while many homeowners found themselves in default, in foreclosure, and on the street. With few exceptions, those who manipulated the system for their own financial benefit were not prosecuted. While there have been occasional instances of accountability where individual executives have been found guilty, they have received less harsh prison sentences than small-time offenders like Michael. No wonder his anger spilled over in his letter to the Pope. No wonder there is so much bitterness concerning our present criminal justice system, where the punishment of many seems grossly unfair compared with the sentences meted out to the rich and powerful.

The avarice behind these schemes would not have surprised Gandhi. There is a political element in the court system, despite the intention of the founding fathers to keep a reasonable separation between the judicial and legislative branches of government. With his legal training, Gandhi was well aware of this danger: "It does not require much reflection to see that it is through the courts that a government establishes its authority, and it is through schools that it manufactures clerks and other employees. They are both healthy institutions when the government in charge of them is, on the whole, just. They are death traps when the government is unjust."

★★★

Given Gandhi's observation, three paragraphs from my letter about the American judicial system, published in the *Syracuse Post-Standard* on May 25, 2006, reflect my concern about the racism and lack of rehabilitation in the prison industry:

> This facility is but a tiny fraction of the 2.2 million individuals now incarcerated in the United States. Our percentage of prison inmates looms greater than that of any other country in the world.
>
> Two-thirds of the 2.2 million are African-Americans or Hispanics, with an increasing number of women among them. More than 1.5 million children have a parent incarcerated; yet, we claim they are our great resource and hope for the country and the world.
>
> We have to ask ourselves: what are we doing with these resources—human, financial, and spiritual? Our

prison system may be seen as a boon industry by a small percentage of people who reap financial gain from construction and maintenance, but it is a bloated failure to know there are other ways to make corrections work for everyone.

For a judge, a combination of humanitarian concerns balanced against a careful view of available evidence marks a truly outstanding magistrate in the minds of defendants, families, and community. The final sentences can be one measure of that humanity. A good amount of discretion has been taken away from judges in recent times, with the passage of mandatory sentencing laws. These require automatic prison terms for those convicted of certain crimes, often drug offenses. In requiring such sentences guidelines, lawmakers diminish the role of judges, especially their opportunity for compassion. This is one reason for the explosion of the prison population in America, with its disproportionate impact on people of color, the poor, and increasingly, on women. Current United States Supreme Court Justice Anthony Kennedy stated his objection to this procedure: "I can accept neither the necessity nor the wisdom of federal mandatory sentences. In too many cases, mandatory minimum sentences are unwise and unjust…The trial judge is the one actor in the system most experienced with exercising discretion in a transparent, open, and reasoned way."

One of the most powerful novels to address this subject is Dostoevsky's *Crime and Punishment,* which combines mystery, psychological drama, and spirituality. The main character is a desperate young man in Russia who thinks he has planned the perfect crime. In the midst of the robbery, he is interrupted, which results in the murder of an old woman pawnbroker and her sister. It is not the police or the criminal investigator who bring about the confession of the perpetrator Raskolnikov, but his own conscience. At the trial, all the circumstances of the crime are taken into consideration, so the sentence is a merciful one—eight years of hard labor in a prison in Siberia. During his incarceration, the constant love of a young woman prompted the stirrings of Raskolnikov's spiritual reconciliation. Dostoyevsky's implication was clear; without the sense of humanity of many of the characters, including the investigator and the judge, the prisoner would not have realized the promise of renewed hope and a new life. Our judicial system needs honesty and a human touch, not mandatory minimum sentences.

Beyond the judiciary, political roles in our country, especially in the legislative and executive branches, have often become tainted because of pressure coming from many places, including, most notably, swollen campaign contributions together with the power of lobbyists. This corruption may be one answer to the question of why so many eligible voters do not exercise this right.

Gandhi's reflection on the political system in India merits serious consideration by Americans. Do the realities of an ever-expanding prison system filled disproportionately with minorities cause moral concern? The scandals in our own time and place, including many politicians catering to special interest groups and corporations reneging on pension promises, give witness to this abuse. While many executives amass fortunes, the raising of the minimum wage rate to approximate living costs is subject to endless debate. Yet, the bailout for troubled financial institutions, even those with questionable behavior, can seemingly happen overnight.

Political Perspectives

One way to contain abuses of political power is to have decisions made at the lowest possible social level. Gandhi favored this idea, as shown from his teaching and adherence to swadeshi—what belongs to one's own country. The concept begins with decision-making at the lowest unit, such as a small village, and encourages all the basic human needs, including social needs, be provided by that entity. For Gandhi, swadeshi extended well beyond the political realm, but it certainly included it.

In some ways, *swadeshi* mirrors a concept called the Principle of Subsidiarity. This concept first appeared in 1931, in a Catholic social encyclical. The basic idea of subsidiarity is that the higher level of organization gives way to the lower level, when the lower level can accomplish the needed task or objective. When this principle is honored in a political system, governments do not overextend their reach, and corruption can be minimized, since more grassroots attention is brought to bear. Control of decisions is limited, so each level of government or other decision-making entity fits into its proper place. Subsidiarity encourages small, voluntary organizations like labor unions to function as intermediaries between the individual and the state.

In 1925 Gandhi served as president of the Congress Party, working to involve a broader base of Indians in the process. He then took a vow of political silence for one year. This was also the time that he also decided to reserve a day of the week for silence. Gandhi sought to empower others to participate, and then he himself took a step back into a more private life.

On February 20, 1947, Prime Minister Clement Attlee announced to the British House of Commons that Britain would leave India no later than June 1948. A new British viceroy, Lord Louis Mountbatten, was appointed as the twentieth and final top administrator in India. It was his task to work out the details, including the timetable for the independence of India. Mountbatten worked diligently with the Indian Congress to achieve a satisfactory arrangement for both Hindu and Muslim constituencies.

It was a moment that should have been joyous for the "Great Soul" who had worked so long and hard for that goal. It was not to be. The celebration turned out to be bitter for Gandhi. The reason: partition, the political decision to establish Pakistan as a separate nation. So it was with great disappointment that Gandhi witnessed the changing political tide.

It was not the British government that drove the wedge between Hindus and Muslims. Notably instead, it was an individual Muslim politician, Mohammad Ali Jinnah. Seven years younger and from the same province as Gandhi, Jinnah came from a wealthy family. After a successful career as a lawyer in London, he returned to India in 1935. Jinnah opposed Gandhi's efforts for a united secular state and looked to develop Pakistan as a separate Muslim state. From the time of their working relationship in the Indian Congress in 1920, when Gandhi had begun pushing for self-rule with one government incorporating all Indian citizens, Jinnah fostered a political separation of Hindu and Muslim constituencies. During their first public disagreements on the issue, Gandhi's position prevailed, but not at the end, when Britain decided to leave India.

In 1944, when it was evident that Britain would soon cede independence to India, serious political discussions were taking place. Gandhi wrote to Jinnah, suggesting talks, signing his letter cordially as "Your brother, Gandhi." Jinnah's response and subsequent correspondence was always written in a formal mode: "Mr. Gandhi." They met personally and corresponded several times, with their entire written exchange being published. The wall between them was the issue of a one-nation solution, a united India, or the two-nation partition.

During the national debate in India's Congress, Jinnah declared a Direct Action Day on August 16, 1946. With that signal, violence flared up between Hindus and Muslims, and soon tragedy became commonplace, especially in the northern regions where Muslims were in a majority. Under the fear of continued violence, the departing British made the decision in favor of two separate nations.

Gandhi's Heartbreak

Riots took place in Calcutta and reached into the villages in the province of Bihar as partition approached. Gandhi was filled with grief, and though seventy-seven years of age, he walked the streets of Calcutta in the company of a respected Muslim leader, where their presence and Gandhi's fasting helped to stem the violence. Then, the Mahatma traveled to a remote area in Northern India, walking to over four dozen remote villages during a four-month period in 1946 and early 1947, while the heated political debate unfolded. During this pilgrimage, he preached nonviolence in every village.

This was an extended period of sadness for Gandhi, seeing many of the ideals and efforts of his lifetime smashed by bloody conflicts between Hindus and Muslims. As an optimist, he continued to recognize and encourage individual efforts of kindness and comradeship among Indians of both religions, so alike in many ways, despite varying beliefs and customs.

Even the political process of implementing partition, once completed in favor of separation of the two bodies, occurred in a premature manner. By his individual decision, Lord Mountbatten moved the original schedule for independence ahead by several months.

On August 15, 1947, India became independent, and Pakistan was created. Gandhi did not celebrate. The bloodbath that followed, as Hindus and Muslims relocated, weighed on Gandhi and the entire Indian population. Rather than allow depression to overwhelm him, however, Gandhi never stopped trying to bridge the widening gap between Hindus and Muslims by focusing on the micro-level of individual relationships. This effort, in the face of the vast migration of Hindus and Sikhs coming out of West Punjab (Pakistan) and the movement of Muslims out of India toward Pakistan, once again gave the world another measure of the character of Gandhi.

Violence erupted in many areas as over fifteen million people joined the exodus. At one point, Gandhi was informed that a single migration line was fifty-seven miles long. The British decision to advance the timing of the independence plan and accept the breakaway of the new Muslim nation proved to be an unmitigated disaster for a vast number of Indians, both Hindus and Muslims. From the very beginning and all through the process, Gandhi stood opposed to the separation. He emerged as a heroic figure, whose position on the matter was recognized, too late, as the correct one.

The cartoon (page 121) showing Gandhi warning against partition in 1947 gives the observer a sense of Gandhi's disappointment and fear. This image helped inform the world of his dissent from the political decision to establish the nation of Pakistan. In the adjustment of the two territories, the slaughter that ensued was a sad witness to Gandhi's warnings and a blow to his efforts to instill a culture of nonviolence throughout India. His lifelong efforts at peacemaking between Hindus and Muslims in a united India came to a crushing impasse. There was nothing self-serving about Gandhi when he originally took up the cause of Hindu-Muslim relationship. Early on, long before any serious discussion of Indian independence, Gandhi knew that the British government often looked to play one religious group against the other in their pursuit of maintaining control over India. Gandhi wanted none of that divisiveness. Even after the momentous political decision of separation had been made, Gandhi continued his individual effort to heal the cultural and religious friction between Muslims and Hindus. Right to the end, at the time of his assassination, he was planning a visit to Pakistan.

Fateful War Decisions

In America, there has thankfully not been a parallel experience of the painful separation of Pakistan and India, although the Civil War was disastrous in its own right. As a country, however, the United States has endured great points of shock. The trauma of September 11, 2001 shook the nation, and to a large extent, the world. After the attack people everywhere were trying to make sense of the tragedy. Instead of declaring a period of national mourning, rather than reflecting on the senselessness and destruction of the violent acts, leaders began looking for ways to retaliate. From the executive branch of government, American citizens were encouraged to return to normal and start spending money again so our capitalist economy could continue to flourish. The drums of war began to beat. Not only was Afghanistan quickly targeted; seeds were planted for a preemptive war in Iraq. Trying to make a connection between 9/11 and Iraq to Congress and the American people, the administration bent over backwards in their contorted reasoning and public statements.

Just as the separation of Pakistan from India brought more violence and a massive migration, so, too, the United States declaring wars in Afghanistan and Iraq have brought about death and destruction for the Afghan and Iraqi people as well as to U.S. and NATO military personnel. A variety of lies and distortions that led to the decision to invade Iraq have eventually come to light. The numberless migration of Iraqi refugees seeking refuge in surrounding countries has received little media attention in comparison with the thousands of deaths of United States military troops. Likewise, the number of Iraqi civilian deaths can only be estimated, but it is known to be in the range of hundreds of thousands.

The Hindu concept of ahimsa gets lost in war. As a consequence of our occupation of Iraq, there are many dimensions of this violence that remain in the shadows. Putting all the effects of war into perspective is difficult. My letter to the editor published in the *Syracuse Post-Standard*, on March 31, 2009, identifies a reason for the confusion:

★★★

'O, what a tangled web we weave when first we practice to deceive.' These words of Sir Walter Scott seem to have a special relevance for our time. Your news story "Memo of Bush-Blair Meeting Shows Early Talk of Iraqi War" made clear Bush's determination to start the war, regardless of the United Nations Security Council discussions or the weapons inspectors' findings.

The memo from January 31, 2003 shows that both the president and prime minister 'acknowledge that no unconventional weapons had been found inside Iraq.' However, that was not what the public or the congress was told at the time.

On March 20 of this year, President Bush made the following statement: 'First, just if I might correct a misconception, I don't think we ever said—at least I know that I didn't say that there was a direct connection between September the 11th and Saddam Hussein.'

In fact, in a letter to the congress on March 21, 2003, two days after the invasion of Iraq, he indicated that the use of armed forces against Iraq is consistent with this linkage. Also, what was Vice-President Cheney telling the nation about this connection again and again, until well after a captured al-Qaida leader admitted that he himself had lied about this linkage to escape torture?

While it now seems impossible for our present government to untangle this web, the American public seems to be awakening to how twisted and knotted official deception has become."

The violence of war leads to other consequences. One of these involves torture. The issues at Abu Ghraib and Guantanamo have brought worldwide attention. When a government flaunts international bans on torture and claims its right to do so, it violates international standards, but it also affects the spiritual life of the country. If the soul of the nation is more than a metaphor, then, complicity in torture methods takes its spiritual toll on the a nation and its citizens. Gandhi believed that the government, in addition to individuals, must develop principles based on truth and honesty. When it fails to do so, the collective psyche of a nation is blighted. The discussion on whether water boarding (simulated drowning) is a form of acceptable torture may seem academic, but it fails the test of truth, honesty, and nonviolence. Indeed, how can torture in any form ever be called acceptable?

If Gandhi were to visit America today, he would likely feel comfortable in the company of those protesting against war, torture, and other violations of human rights. He might agree that such efforts at present seem futile and the odds for success feel overwhelming, but he would assure activists that their witness is necessary to tell the rest of the country that we can do better. As for the political process, judging from his encouragement of villagers to participate in the All India Congress, Gandhi would encourage involvement, especially on the grassroots, local level.

We can guess that the increased political involvement of young people and other newly registered voters in 2008 would be an encouraging sign for Gandhi. Likewise, many of the pledges and idealism that Obama brought to his presidential campaign would resonate with Gandhi, as it did in actuality with people from many quarters throughout the world.

However, Gandhi would probably express caution, knowing that the answers to deep problems are often beyond the reach of purely political solutions. He would likely share that in his own satyagraha campaigns he often questioned his own judgment on whether day-to-day decisions were faithful to the principles he proclaimed.

With the unfolding knowledge of how far greed and corruption have been woven into the social fabric of the corporate and political life of many decision makers in the United States, Gandhi might share his view of the common good. This would include keeping a sharp eye on the principles of ahimsa, *moksha* (liberation for all), sacrifice, and a willingness to suffer for a good cause. He would likely bring us back to some basic principles of trust in government and insist that politics can be a good profession, but acknowledge that it takes courage to face the needed radical changes.

> "We consider that the political life of the country will become thoroughly corrupt if we import western tactics and methods. We believe that nothing but the strictest adherence to honesty, fair play, and charity can advance the true interests of the country." —Gandhi

Eight

Final Word

The indicator reading final spin on a washing machine in the Canaan Federal Prison Camp was a signal to waiting inmates that a machine would soon be available. The notion of spin takes on a different meaning in political and media circles. Unwelcome political news is often fed to the general public with a spin to make it palatable. Gandhi never deliberately placed a spin on his articles. He was not afraid of sharing the unvarnished truth, even though at times it placed him in an unfavorable light. He knew the value of the printed word, and he used it to promote and clarify his position on many of the far-ranging issues of his day.

Gandhi printed the list of social sins and tried to live by them. To probe the social dimensions of each of the seven principles and to examine them in the perspective of one's own journey takes moral courage. Gandhi had that courage and tried to avoid the traps of any of the seven sins on the list. In various ways, Gandhi confronted his own weaknesses.

★★★

In my high school days, I was introduced to this subject of social sins through the Catholic Interracial Council in Syracuse.

It was my first experience considering racial issues beyond individual faults. In later studies, the concept of a sin as something beyond a personal failing became more apparent to me through studying social encyclicals of the Church and other justice issues, like the rights of workers to organize collectively, the qualified right to private property, issues of war and peace, and the arms race.

One example of a localized social issue helped me make a connection to swadeshi. Over a quarter-century ago, I was approached by a small group of nuns who were renting a house in a poor neighborhood. Having taken the vows of poverty, they were prevented from purchasing the property, yet at the same time, they wished to continue their ministry in that community. In talking over their request with others, one suggested the idea of an urban land trust. I convened a few friends to consider the idea. Over several morning meetings at a local diner, the plan took shape. We envisioned that, once established, it would allow us to hold property in stewardship that would assist the sisters' need, do renovation work on other structures, and invite families to live in these homes. Our idea was to connect individual churches to support the families in those renovated houses. In 1981, we incorporated our fledgling organization as "Time of Jubilee."

A few years later, a group of interracial downtown clergy asked to partner with our efforts. We agreed, since it would give us additional moral and financial support from several religious denominations. Since the land-trust structure did not easily fit into existing modes of business, it took some serious negotiating with local banks. Little by little, the group began constructing new homes. Today, there are close to a hundred new single-family dwellings in what was formerly a run-down neighborhood. Renovation work on existing homes has also taken place. A former adult movie house in the area has been shut down, and Spirit of Jubilee Park has replaced a former "shooting gallery" for drug users. A large grocery store, missing in that neighborhood for decades, is in the planning stages. The people who live here, along with city officials, worked together to make the whole area a better place in which to live.

★★★

In both South Africa and India, Gandhi examined and faced the issues that included dimensions of social sins. He addressed them not only with action, but also with the written word. His involvement in the labor dispute in the 1917 mill workers' strike at Ahmadabad is one example of how he utilized the press. Even though many of the mill workers were illiterate, Gandhi distributed fliers and statements daily. The few workers and organizers who were literate read the material to others. Again and again, he used this method to promote and clarify his position on many of the crucial issues of his day. He took pains to respond to his personal mail, which was often voluminous. He opened up schools for children at Tolstoy Farm and in the rural Champaran district in India.

Gandhi's willingness to expose his views in writing often cost him dearly. At the height of his struggle for India's independence, he published three articles in *Young India* stating his open defiance of the British government and encouraging noncooperation, and was arrested for sedition. In the trial, Gandhi summed up the ways that the British occupation had harmed the Indian people and concluded, "it has been a precious privilege for me to be able to write what I have in the various articles tendered in evidence against me…In my opinion, noncooperation with evil is as much a duty as cooperation with good." The judge sentenced Gandhi to six years in prison. Gandhi then thanked the judge for his respect throughout the trial.

It is not difficult to understand why the seven social sins would appeal to Gandhi. He shared some of his own wealth, supported a printing press, divested a lucrative law practice, and turned to farming. In his own life, he modeled the discipline needed to reject the social sin of pleasure without conscience; his lifelong fasting periods bear witness to this trait. In his embrace of swadeshi, Gandhi brought an ethical perspective to commerce and free-trade issues. Although he initially struggled with the morality of war, Gandhi's condemnation of aggression, armed defense and nuclear weapons helped clarify for others the salient issues of present-day conflicts.

Gandhi's belief in the need for sacrifice, his respect for the truths to be found in all major religions, and his vision of himself as a change agent from a spiritual background provides a grounding in understanding his life and work. "God is truth," Gandhi said again and again. In his belief in a personal, caring God he diverged from traditional Hindu beliefs. The daily communal prayer services in his ashrams that drew from a variety of faith traditions gave testimony to his personal foundation. Addressing the social dimension of sin flowed naturally from his deep spirituality. Finally, although reluctantly, Gandhi's willingness to enter the political realm and his belief in principles of truthfulness and honesty within demonstrated that politics can be an honorable profession.

Gandhi has left the world a legacy of the fruits of nonviolence. Although often unsure of what the results would be, he understood the healing power that can come from humanely respectful tactics carried out with strength. That was the truth force of the many satyagraha movements. Moreover, Gandhi's pursuit of truth in his own life allowed him to forgive himself for failures with his own family as well as mistakes in strategy, especially when they involved the suffering of his own followers. Often, he misplaced a trust in political leaders and in some of his own comrades. However, his forgiveness and his belief in nonviolence always allowed him to recover and to move on in the struggle. Such quality and stature also led others to forgive him and to respect him deeply as their Mahatma.

In considering Gandhi's personal austerity and his deep involvement in social issues, his sense of humor can easily be overlooked. It was a hallmark of his life in the ashrams, and it endeared him to many of the women in those settings. Erik Erikson, a renowned psychologist, refers to his humor as "Gandhi's Franciscan gaiety," which persisted even when he was in prison. Erickson's psychological study of Gandhi includes an extended look at his childhood and the abrupt transition from a childhood's carefree development in his first twelve years of age to the sudden burden of adult responsibilities at the time of his marriage. Fortunately, as an adult, he was able to recover his sense of playfulness. Erickson believes that this aspect of his personality was a significant factor in his development, including his commitment to nonviolence.

The effect of Gandhi's self-sacrifice and the power of his witness were not always evident during his lifetime. However, many Indian politicians and common people did acknowledge their value and try to follow his lead. Gandhi described himself as an optimist, and he was generally cheerful and easy to be around. Yet, towards the end of his life he often felt discouragement and personal failure. This was true when violence erupted between Muslims and Hindus and when, despite much of Gandhi's life's work for India's unity and independence, the partition of India and Pakistan occurred.

Gandhi was frequently invited to visit the United States. Various individuals and representatives from different groups came to visit or wrote him letters of invitation. He did not accept them, indicating that the work he had to do in India was quite enough. If he had visited, this man who stood only 5'5" tall, weighed some 110 pounds and dressed in simple, homespun cloth would have undoubtedly been well received, far more than just a curiosity. His message to America likely would have been as critical as his advice when he visited England in 1931 and 1946. Gandhi would have surely enjoyed the people he met in America, flashed his humor, and appreciated every offer of hospitality. Yet, he might have found race relations, blatantly deceptive advertising, excessive profit taking, and intervention in the affairs of other countries to be troubling. He would not have hesitated to address these issues publicly.

Despite never visiting its shores, Gandhi's teachings and examples have reached America. They have, in truth, reached the entire world. The recent acknowledgement of the United Nations General Assembly in choosing Gandhi's birthday as the International Day of Peace and Nonviolence would seem to validate the conclusion of leaders of every nation that nonviolence is possible for individuals and societies. It is the world's hope!

> "We may never be strong enough to be entirely nonviolent in thought, word, and deed. But we must keep nonviolence as our goal and make strong progress toward it. The

attainment of freedom, whether for a person, a nation, or a world, must be in exact proportion to the attainment of nonviolence for each." —Gandhi

Sources

Introduction: Gandhi's List of Social Sins

GhandiServe Foundation—www.gandhiserve.org Photo: Kanu Gandhi/GandhiServe

Gandhi. Produced and directed by Richard Attenborough. 2 hr. 35 min. Columbia Pictures, 1982. DVD.

http://www.soaw.org. Website for the school of the Americas Watch.

Newsweek. "Running a School for Dictators." August 9, 2003.

Klein, Naomi. "'Never Before!' Our Amnesiac Torture Debate." *The Nation*. December 26, 2005, 11-12.

Ingram, Catherine. *In the Footsteps of Gandhi: Conversations With Spiritual Social Activists*.

Berkeley, CA: Parallax Press, 2003. Includes a dozen interviews with notable individuals whose lives were influenced by Gandhi, 9-11, 76-130, 224-254.

Young India. October 22, 1925. List of seven social sins.

Pope Pius XI. Papal Documents. *Quadragesimo anno, Acta Apostolica Sedis*. Rome, Italy: Vatican Polyglot Press, 1931.

Fisher, Louis. *The Essential Gandhi, His Life Work and Ideas*. New York: Alfred Knopf, 1962.

"'I tell you, I was permitted,'" 36.

Gandhi's, Arun and Sunanda with Yellin, Carol Lynn. *The Forgotten Woman; The Untold Story of Kastur, Wife of*

Mahatma Gandhi. Huntsville, AR: Ozark Mountain Press, 1998. 167, Statistics regarding the jail terms of the Gandhi family in South Africa.

Erikson, Erik. *Gandhi's Truth; On the Origins of Militant Nonviolence.* (New York: W.W. Norton Company, 1969.) The four-fold ruin of India and Nehru's reference to Gandhi.

The Rainbow. Vol.13, no 1. Bell Multicultural High School, Washington DC. January 2005.

Woolever, Frank. "Prison Memoirs" *The Catholic Sun*, August 9, 2003. *The Catholic Sun* is the official newspaper of the Catholic diocese of Syracuse, New York.

Andrews, Charles F. *Mahatma Gandhi, His Life and Ideas* Mumbai: Jaico Publishing House, 2005. Includes a short list of common Indian words associated with Gandhi's work.

Gandhi in the Lion's Den; *Simplicissimus*, Munich (Germany)—Copyright: Vithalbhal Jhavert/Gandhi Serve—KW: Mahatma Gandhi

Chapter One: Wealth Without Work

Fischer, Louis. *The Essential Gandhi, His Life, Work and Ideas.* New York: Alfred Knopf, 1962. "We should spin," 223.

Ruskin, John. *Unto This Last.* London: Smith, Elder and Co., 65, Cornhill, 1862.

Fischer, "Everything from cooking to scavenging," 103.

Fischer. Silence of Trappist monks, 239.

Woolever, Frank. *"*Messing With Success.*" The Post Standard*, Syracuse, NY, February 20, 2005.

_____. "Wealth Without Work." *The Catholic Sun*, September 28, 2006.

Dunbar, Leslie. *The Common Interest.* New York: Pantheon Books, 1988.

Woolever, Frank. Personal letter to Patricia Tappan, New York State Commissioner of Corrections. October 15, 1999.

Bronfenbrenner, Urie. *The Ecology of Human Development: Experiments by Nature and Design*. Cambridge, MA: Harvard University Press, 1979. xii.

Fischer, Louis. *Life of Mahatma Gandhi*. New York: Harper & Row, 1950. The story of Gandhi's first public fast and the dynamics of the workers' strike in Ahmadabad.

Mathews, Robert Guy. *Wall Street Journal*, August 31, 2005. Statistics on CEO pay.

Kristof, Nicholas D. "Equality, a True Soul Food." *The New York Times*, January 1, 2011. Statistics on wealth inequality.

Wilson, William J. "Perspective on the Ecology of Human Development." Symposium at Cornell University, September 28, 1993.

Erikson, Erik. *Gandhi's Truth; On the Origins of Militant Nonviolence*. New York: W.W. Norton Company, 1969. Nehru's quote, 272.

Rynne, Terrence. *Gandhi & Jesus: The Saving Power of Nonviolence*. Maryknoll, NY: Orbis, 2008. Idea that religion was a constant for Gandhi.

Indian Opinion, March 18, 1905. "An infallible test of civilization,"

Gandhiji's Ten Commandments; 1928. Copyright: Vithalbhal Jhavert/Gandhi Server—KW: Mahatma Gandhi

Chapter Two: Pleasure Without Conscience

Peacemaking Day by Day. Vol. I. Erie, PA Pax Christi USA, 1989. "It is good enough to talk of God," 53.

Ingram, Catherine. *In the Footsteps of Gandhi; Conversations with Spiritual Activists*. Berkeley, CA: Parallax Press, 2003. Interview with Hanh. 76-95.

Fischer, Louis. *The Essential Gandhi, His Life Work and Ideas*. New York: Allied Knopf, 1962. "who has not mastered his palate," 243.

_____. "Hold alike pleasures and pain." Quote from the Gita, 183.

Gandhi, Arun, Sunanda Gandhi, and Carol Lynn Yellin. *The Forgotten Woman; The Untold Story of Kastur, Wife of Mahatma Gandhi*. Huntsville, AR: Ozark Mountain Press, 1998. This book presents an insightful picture of Arun's grandmother, who was an intimate part of Gandhi's life during their sixty-two years of marriage and a source of inspiration for many Indian women.

Fischer, Louis. The Life of Mahatma Gandhi. New York: Harper and Row, 1950. Description of the content of *From Yeravda Mandir,* the booklet Gandhi wrote in Yeravda jail concerning the nature of God and the ideal conduct of man, including truth, love and chastity, 300-305.

Woolever, Frank. "First Impressions of Federal Prison: What a Waste." *The Post Standard*, Syracuse, NY. May 25, 2006.

_____. "Pleasure Without Conscience." *The Catholic Sun*, October 5, 2006.

Ingram, Catherine, *In the Footsteps of Gandhi; Conversations with Spiritual Activists*. Parallax Press, 2003. Interview with Chavez, 97-115.

Erikson, Erik. *Gandhi's Truth; On the Origins of Militant Nonviolence*. New York: W.W. Norton Company, 1969. Erickson's quotes extensively from Gandhi's autobiography, *The Story of My Experiment with Truth*. Observation on Gandhi's installment writing of his autobiography, 61.

Andrews, Charles F. *Mahatma Gandhi, His Life and Ideas*. Mumbai: Jaico Publishing House, 2005. Gandhi's address to a Christian Missionary Conference, 77.

Indian Opinion, August 26, 1905. "Happiness, the goal,"

Gandhi & Co. Salt; 1930. Copyright: Vithalbhal Jhavert/Gandhi Server—KW: Mahatma Gandhi

Chapter Three: Commerce Without Morality

Indian Opinion. October 15, 1904. "Herein is a practical lesson,"

Ingram, Catherine. *In the Footsteps of Gandhi; Conversations with Spiritual Activists*. Berkeley, CA: Parallax Press, 2003. Interview with Ariyante, 117-130.

Andrews, Charles F. *Mahatma Gandhi, His Life and Ideas*. Mumbai: Jaico Publishing House, 2005. Quote on swadeshi, 76.

Chadha, Yogesh. *Gandhi, a Life*. Hoboken, NJ: Wiley & Sons, 1998. Authors who influenced Gandhi during his time in England, 159. Connection to Rustin, 104.

Fischer, Louis. *Life of Mahatma Gandhi*. New York: Harper & Row Publishers, 1950. Quote from *Hind Swaraj*. 125.

www.witnessfor peace.org. Witness for Peace is an organization that aims at promoting political transparencies in Latin American countries. WFP's mission is to support peace, justice and sustainable economies in the Americas by changing U.S. policies and corporate practices which contribute to poverty and oppression in Latin America and the Caribbean.

Woolever, Frank. "Time is Ripe to Forgive Debt: Jubilee Concept for Struggling Countries Merits Action." *The Post-Standard*, Syracuse, NY, October 10, 1999.

_____. "Commerce Without Morality." *The Catholic Sun*, October 12, 2006.

Polgreen, Lydia & Simons Marlise "Global Sludge Ends in Tragedy for Ivory Coast." *International Herald-Tribune*. October 2, 2006.

Woolever, Frank. "Menchu's Life Reflects Native People's Plight." *The Post-Standard*, Syracuse, NY, December 23, 1992.

Mander, Jerry & Tauli-Corpuz, Victoria, Ed. *Paradigm Wars; Indigenous Peoples' Resistance to Globalization*. (San Francisco, CA: Sierra Club Books, 2006.)

_____. "Community Sharing One Skin" by Jeanette Armstrong, 238.

Lyons, Oren, Chief. *Haudenosaunee Statement*. 7th Session of the Permanent Form on Indigenous Issues, United Nations, New York, N.Y., April 21-May 3, 2008. The entire statement can be obtained by mail by contacting the American Indian Law Alliance, 11 Broadway Avenue, New York, N.Y. 10004, or by e-mail by contacting aila@ailanyc.org.

_____. Speech. UN Millennium World Peace Summit of Religious and Spiritual Leaders, 2000.

Fischer, Louis. Gandhi's complete letter to Lord Irwin, 265-267.

Gandhi, Arun, Sunanda Gandhi, and Carol Lynn Yellin. *The Forgotten Woman; The Untold Story of Kastur, Wife of Mahatma Gandhi*. Huntsville, AR: Ozark Mountain Press, 1998. The description of the march to the sea, 252.

Young India. January 5, 1922. "India's greatest glory,"

Peacemaking Day by Day. Erie, PA: Pax Christi, USA, 1989. Gandhi's speech at the *Christian Missionary Conference*. Madras, India. February 14, 1916. "India need not be drawn," 6.

Lord Willingdon's Dilemma. *Hindustan Times*,1933. Copyright: Vithalbhal Jhavert/Gandhi Server—KW: Mahatma Gandhi

Chapter Four: Science Without Humanity

Young India. May 6, 1926.

Andrews, Charles F. *Mahatma Gandhi, His Life and Ideas*. Mumbai: Jaico Publishing House, 2005. 129-131, Gandhi's Confession of Faith, written in 1909, is quoted in its entirety.

Gandhi, Mahatma. *Non-Violence in Peace and War*..Garland Publishing, 1972. "What difference does it make to the dead?"

Haring, Bernard. *The Healing Power of Peace and Nonviolence*. Middlegreen, Slough SL3 6 BT, England, 1986. 5.

Butler, Smedley D., Brigadier General. *War is a Racket*. Los Angeles, CA: Feral House, 2003. The Butler family published the first edition in 1935.

Young India. July 17, 1924. "They say 'means are,"

Pax Christi International is a non-profit, non-governmental Catholic peace movement working on a global scale on a wide variety of issues in the fields of human rights, human security, disarmament and demilitarization, just world order and religion and violent conflict.

Dear, John, Rev. S.J. Interview with Philip Berrigan. *The Life of Resistance: A Conversation With Philip Berrigan.* Oakland, California. 1993

McAlister, Liz. "*Phil Berrigan's Statement Before Death.*" . 2002.

Day, Dorothy. *The Catholic Worker.* 1945.

McSorely, Richard, S.J. It's a Sin to Build a Nuclear Weapon. Baltimore, MD: Fortkamp Publishing, 1991.

Woolever, Frank. "Nuclear Club Members Lack Moral Authority" *The Post Standard*, Syracuse, NY. August 23, 2005.

_____."Violence Provides No Closure: Pan-Am 103 Tragedy May Be Part of Vicious Circle." *The Post Standard*, Syracuse, NY. December 29, 1998.

_____. "Science Without Humanity." *The Catholic Sun*, October 19, 2006.

Bult-Ito, Abel. "Nothing Depleted About Depleted Uranium" . January 22, 2006.

Gritz, Jennie Rothenberg. "The African in Him" *The Atlantic.* January 5, 2009.

Thurman, Howard. *Jesus and the Disinherited.* Boston, MA: Beacon Press, 1976. 84.

May, Rollo. *Power and Innocence: a Search for the Sources of Violence.* New York: Dell 1972. 166.

Harijan. July 11, 1946. "So far as I can see,"

Kelly, Kathy et.al. *Voices for Creative Nonviolence Newsletter.* August, 2009. . VCN runs strategic campaigns and experiments in truth engaging in active nonviolent resistance. Such resistance must take into account that war-making is both military and economic.1249 W. Argyle Street, Chicago, IL, 60640.

Bill Moyers Journal. Television show. "Is a Military Strategy the Best Option in Afghanistan?" Interview with Pierre Sprey. January 30, 2009. Sprey, former Pentagon planner, discussed drones, and the impossibility of gaining Afghan supporters while killing civilians.

Peabody, Elizabeth, Ed. Æsthetic Papers. The Editor, Boston, 1849. Includes *Civil Disobedience* by Henry David Thoreau.

Harijan. July 7, 1946. "The moral to be legitimately drawn,"

Gandhi on Elephant. *Kladderadatsch*, 1922. Copyright: Vithalbhal Jhavert/Gandhi Server—KW: Mahatma Gandhi

Chapter Five: Knowledge Without Character

Young India. August 4, 1920. "There are moments,"
Young India, September 10, 1931. "I shall work for an India,"
Andrews, Charles F. *Mahatma Gandhi, His Life and Ideas*. Mumbai: Jaico Publishing House, 2005. Metaphor of hand representing Gandhi's comprehensive program for central unity in India, 238.
Fischer, Louis. *The Life of Mahatma Gandhi*. New York: Harper and Row, 1950. G.K. Gokhale, was a revered leader of the Indian Nationalist movement and Gandhi's mentor, 108.
Ingram, Catherine, Ed. *In the Footsteps of Gandhi; Conversations with Spiritual Activists.*. Berkeley, CA: Parallax Press, 2003. Interview with Brother David Steindl-Rast. 229-233.
Woolever, Frank. "A Friend Remembers Father McVey." *The Catholic Sun*. May 4, 1995.
_____. "Knowledge Without Character" *The Catholic Sun*, October 26, 2006.
Vanier, Jean. *Community and Growth*. Toronto, ON: Novalis, 1989. Vanier is the author of many books and publications; among the most well known is *Community and Growth*. Access to all of Vanier's writings can be gained through the L'Arche Collection from Novalis Publishing, 49 Front Street, East Toronto, Ontario, MSE 1B3, Canada or The Consortium Publishing Company, 370 Lexington Avenue, New York, NY 10017.
_____. *Letters of L'Arche*. December 2005.
Andrews, Charles F. *Mahatma Gandhi, His Life and Ideas*. Mumbai: Jaico Publishing House, 2005. Gandhi's quote on fearlessness, 67.
Young India. June 17, 1926. "Strength in numbers,"
We Have Different Weapons. 1930. Copyright: Vithalbhal Jhavert/Gandhi Server — KW: Mahatma Gandhi

Chapter Six: Worship Without Sacrifice

Young India. December 6, 1928. "Let no one for a moment,"
Young India. July 7, 1927. "No doubt religion needs,"
Woolever, Frank. "Seeking to Live in Harmony" *The Post Standard*, Syracuse, NY. August 25, 2006.
Andrews, Charles F. *Mahatma Gandhi, His Life and Ideas*. Mumbai: Jaico Publishing House, 2005. The quotes from Tagore's letter to Gandhi,184.
Rynne, Terrence J. Maryknoll, New York, Orbis Books, 2008. Quote regarding Jesus' way of living, 112, Quote by John Howard Yoder, 149.
Andrews. Gandhi's adherence to swadeshi, 111.
Fischer, Louis. *The Essential Gandhi, His Life Work and Ideas*. New York: Alfred Knopf, 1962. The author spent a week with Gandhi at his ashram in 1942
Fischer, Louis. *Life of Mahatma Gandhi*. New York: Harper & Row Publishers, 1950. Tagore's statement on Gandhi's prolonged fast, 311.
Rynne, Terrence J. *Gandhi & Jesus; The Saving Power of Nonviolence*. Maryknoll, NY: Orbis, 2008. Reference to Charles Andrews and Andrews quote, 87.
Tolstoy, Leo. *The Kingdom of God is Within You*. Lincoln: University of Nebraska Press, 1984.
_____. *Resurrection*. New York: New American Library, 1899.
Erikson, Erik. *Gandhi's Truth; On the Origins of Militant Nonviolence*. New York: W.W. Norton Company, 1969. Gandhi's consideration of converting to Christianity.
Fischer, Louis. *The Essential Gandhi, His Life Work and Ideas*. New York: Alfred Knopf, 1962. Implications of the Rowlatt Act, 176.
Gandhi, Arun, Sunanda Gandhi, and Carol Lynn Yellin. *The Forgotten Woman; The Untold Story of Kastur, Wife of Mahatma Gandhi*. Huntsville, AR: Ozark Mountain Press, 1998. The Rowlett Act, 232.

Fischer, Louis. *Life of Mahatma Gandhi.* New York: Harper & Row Publishers, 1950. Lord Reading's letter to his son, 195-6.

Young India, January 12, 1921. "Noncooperation is not a movement,"

Bourgeois, Roy. Letter to the author. April 30, 2006.

Dearden, John, Cardinal. Homily November, 1979. Romero shared these words, and they are often attributed to him, but they come from a homily Cardinal Dearden gave at a Mass for deceased priests. These words were drafted for Cardinal Dearden by Ken Untener.

Zachmer, R.C., Ed. *The Concise Encyclopedia of Living Faiths.* New York: Hawthorn Books, 1959. The question of the long-range impact of Gandhi on South Africa and India is not easy to measure. The dramatic events in South Africa, after their independence, give a clue to the answer, with the reconciliation process the prime exhibit. An indication of Gandhi's effect on India can be seen in this book. Although published only twelve years after Gandhi's death, Professor A. L. Basham describes the changes in the Hindu culture and religious life, including the social advances by Untouchables. This British professor of the history of South Asia is also able to place Gandhi within the larger context of Hinduism, 225-260.

Ingram, Catherine, Ed. *In the Footsteps of Gandhi; Conversations with Spiritual Activists.* Parallax Press, 2003. Interview with Desmond Tutu, 249-254.

Woolever, Frank. "That Time Again." *The Catholic Sun.* September 25, 2008

Fischer, Louis. *The Essential Gandhi, His Life Work and Ideas.* "My sympathies are all," 328.

Carroll, James. *Constantine's Sword; The Church and the Jews.* Boston, MA: Houghton Mifflin Company, 2001.

Pope Benedict XVI, *Summorum Pontificum.* July 7, 2007

Peacemaking Day By Day, Vol. I. Erie, PA: Pax Christi USA, 1989. "The only people on Earth,"

Danger Signal, 1947.Copyright: Vithalbhal Jhavert/Gandhi Server—KW: Mahatma Gandhi

Chapter Seven: Politics Without Principle

Young India. April 28, 1920. "I believe that it is possible,"

King, Martin Luther, Jr. *National Pubic Radio. All Things Considered.* January 16, 2009. King's 1959 radio address to India after a one-month visit.

Fischer, Louis. *Life of Mahatma Gandhi.* New York: Harper & Row Publishers, 1950. "Hitherto, it has been a struggle," 223.

Young India. June 8, 1925." By a long process"

Hedges, Chris. *Losing Moses on the Freeway.* New York: Free Press, 2005. 131-132, 157-169.

Woolever, Frank. "First Impressions of Federal Prison: What a Waste." *The Post Standard,* Syracuse, NY. May 25, 2006.

Dostoevski, Fyodor. *Crime and Punishment.* Oxford : Oxford University Press, 1988.

Curran, Charles E. *Catholic Social Teaching, 1891-Present; A Historical, Theological and Ethical Analysis.* Washington, DC: Georgetown University Press, 2002. The principle of subsidiarity receives a full exposition in this book.

Woolever, Frank. "Bush Wove Tangled Web With Iraq Weapons Deceit." *The Post-Standard,* Syracuse, NY March 31, 2009.

_____. "Politics Without Principle." *The Catholic Sun,* November 9, 2006.

Rynne, Terrence J. *Gandhi and Jesus; The Saving Power of Nonviolence.* Maryknoll, New York: Orbis, 2008. References to moksha, 33, 36.

Young India. January 14, 1920. "We consider that the political life,"

Chapter Eight: Final Word

Fischer, Louis. *Life of Mahatma Gandhi.* New York: Harper & Row Publishers, 1950. Gandhi's statement in court, 203.

Erikson, Erik. *Gandhi's Truth; On the Origins of Militant Nonviolence.* New York: W.W. Norton Company, 1969. 133, The observations on Gandhi's sense of humor.

Peacemaking Day by Day, Vol. 1. Erie, PA: Pax Christi USA, 1989. "We may never be strong enough,"